Aware in a World Asleep

A Principled Way for Living Spiritually

First published by O Books, 2010
O Books is an imprint of John Hunt Publishing Ltd., The Bothy, Deershot Lodge, Park Lane, Ropley,
Hants, SO24 0BE, UK
office1@o-books.net
www.o-books.net

Distribution in:	South Africa
	Stephan Phillips (pty) Ltd
UK and Europe	Email: orders@stephanphillips.com
Orca Book Services	Tel: 27 21 4489839 Telefax: 27 21 4479879
orders@orcabookservices.co.uk	
Tel: 01202 665432 Fax: 01202 666219	Text copyright Jim Young 2008
Int. code (44)	
	Design: Stuart Davies
USA and Canada	
NBN	ISBN: 978 1 84694 261 7
custserv@nbnbooks.com	
Tel: 1 800 462 6420 Fax: 1 800 338 4550	All rights reserved. Except for brief quotations
	in critical articles or reviews, no part of this
Australia and New Zealand	book may be reproduced in any manner without
Brumby Books	prior written permission from the publishers.
sales@brumbybooks.com.au	
Tel: 61 3 9761 5535 Fax: 61 3 9761 7095	The rights of Jim Young as author have been
	asserted in accordance with the Copyright,
Far East (offices in Singapore, Thailand,	Designs and Patents Act 1988.
Hong Kong, Taiwan)	
Pansing Distribution Pte Ltd	
kemal@pansing.com	A CIP catalogue record for this book is available
Tel: 65 6319 9939 Fax: 65 6462 5761	from the British Library.

Printed by Digital Book Print

O Books operates a distinctive and ethical publishing philosophy in
all areas of its business, from its global network of authors to
production and worldwide distribution.

Aware in a World Asleep

A Principled Way for
Living Spiritually

Jim Young

BOOKS

Winchester, UK
Washington, USA

"Jim Young offers an illuminated path to that elusive 'essence' we've been searching for. *Awake in a World Asleep* is accessible, real and inspiring."
Nouk Sanchez & Tomas Vieira, *Take Me To Truth; Undoing the Ego*

"Jim Young takes the spiritual pilgrim on a twenty-first century journey into the world of metaphysics and metaphor—he challenges the seeker to look within, not beyond, for the road map."
Author Jenny Wagget, *The Awakening Dream*, a novel for young adults.

"A much-needed and insightful exploration of finding our inner strength and contributing it to the world."
Author Annie Woods, *Journeys to Places Out of Bounds*

"Young's writings have inspired my own sense of Spirituality, which in turn has inspired my art."
Stephen Sumner, artist and art educator.

"Dr. Young teaches that when we learn to let go of the ego-intellect so that our Spirit is manifested we live as the 'masters' we were created to be."
Dr. Charles and Ramona McNeal, facilitators, A Course in Miracles, and program coordinators, Unitarian Universalist Church, Eureka Springs, AR

"Jim Young's writing has helped me know that the Divine Within is where it's at! God is. There is no more." Marsha Havens, Cofounder of the Arkansas Metaphysical Society and President of the Christian Science Society of Eureka Springs, AR

Jim Young's Website

www.creationspirit.net contains additional creations to come through Jim Young, including E-books and a link to his collector quality photography. Speaking services and classes dealing with his writings are also available. Contact Jim at: creationspirit@gmail.com.

Books by Jim Young

"The righteous man is not an individual who thinks he knows what is best for the nation; rather the righteous man is one who is sure he does not know and is willing to 'be still and know I am God.' This is enough to know, and then *let* this knowing do the work. 'Ye shall know the truth and the truth shall make you free.'"

Joel A. Goldsmith

Contents

Acknowledgments

I dedicate *Aware in a World Asleep* to the consciousness of inner Wisdom. I heartily do so in my awareness of its creative power and demonstration of perfection. I do so also to affirm the clarity and purpose that inner Wisdom is for the spiritual journey.

It is through the inner Wisdom we hold in common that we experience. Spiritually we come alive by becoming aware of the still, small voice and expressing or demonstrating its Wisdom endlessly. It is this level of demonstration that spiritually defines eternity, immortality, and infinity lived. While expressing what we are as One, duality ceases to be. With ever-lasting gratitude for the gifts revealed through the still, small voice of Wisdom, I am dedicated to allowing creation to manifest endlessly from this only true source for the good of the Universe.

Also, I take this opportunity to express deep gratitude to a cadre of faithful and talented readers and authors in their own right, Sparo Arika Vigil, Marguerite Burgin, Jenny Wagget and Livea Perish. Their skillful and sensitive editing has helped shape spiritual depth and meaning. To be sure, publisher John Hunt has guided me wisely and most encouragingly, as well as providing both challenge and inspiration, and for that I am ever grateful.

Thanks, too, to Stuart Davies, Nick Welch and Trevor Greenfield of O-Books for the creative talents they have applied to the production of this book. I am also grateful to Todd Young, Todd Young Studio, for inspiring the book cover into being.

Last, and certainly not least, I thank my immediate and extended family, as well as those who have supported these offerings through their own enjoyment of them.

Jim Young

Introduction

If you're feeling that you are "in this world but not of it," this is a sure calling to spiritual awareness. Essentially, the world we see around us today is an illusion, a dream repeatedly depicted out of a complex, erroneous set of beliefs and opinions found outside ourselves.

Inner experience has shown me that our purpose in Life is to become aware of our inherent Wisdom and to express our awareness of its gifts as our moment-to-moment guide. I invite you to an exploration of what mirrors Wisdom for you, leading to a principled path of spiritual awareness. Spiritual awareness requires a willingness to consider new ways of viewing Life and our place in it. It also requires that we use outward appearance as a reflection of the current state of our spiritual awareness. We mutually serve one another as models for arriving at spiritual demonstration. We truly are mirrors for each other of our inner condition. We are lent to one another this way.

Aware in a World Asleep is about becoming aware of the erroneous thought process that erects a veil between our spiritual Truth and the illusions of the ego dream. In this pursuit we are awakened to a deeper experience of Life itself. From this deeper experience we come to awareness of Wisdom's meaning, for us. Entertaining new perspectives and a willingness to honor intuitive perceptions can be helpful. As you proceed, do not be at all concerned that you might not be ready to engage with this topic as one would hope. Indeed, if you just consider each new perspective with an open mind as you go along, spiritual awareness will take on the fullness of its intended meaning for you by the time you reach the end.

Once we find ourselves experiencing the voice found in Wisdom, we come to understand there is only one way to that Truth. This understanding leads us to experience Oneness, which replaces the illusions of duality that have been inflicted on us over the centuries through the collective consciousness.

In the following chapters, a basic approach to experiencing Wisdom as inner Truth is described. It leads from a basic philosophical foundation to the identification of what continues to distract us from seeing and living our spiritual reality. Such distractions fall away from our daily routine as we practice listening inwardly. The outcome? Spiritual reality replaces the illusions of duality and we are free to live the one and only path of inner Truth.

Of course, as we become aware of new spiritual Truths, we come closer to anchoring conscious awareness as a way of Life on a moment-to-moment basis. At the end of the book you will find a section entitled BEING ON YOUR WAY, which spells out some exercises related to each of the seven principles for living spiritually. I'm confident that you will think of even more of your own as you proceed with these suggestions. The key is to practice diligently, so your new habits can quickly replace the old.

Also, around and about you'll find stories and examples sprinkled throughout the text. These are intended to loosen the hold we have on current beliefs, opinions and habits, so we can make more room for the resonance of our inner Truth. Here's a brief example, which helps focus spiritual purpose.

"When as a young man, I wanted to change the world. I found it was difficult to change the world, so I tried to change my nation. When I found I couldn't change the nation, I began to change my town. I couldn't change the town, and as an older man, I tried to change my family. Now, as an old man, I realize the only thing I can change is myself, and suddenly realized that if long ago I had changed myself, I could have made an impact on my family. My family and I could have made an impact on our town. Their impact could have changed the nation, and I could indeed have changed the world."

Author unknown

My own life gives testimony to this story. As each of us travels our spiritual journey, we become adept at its ways. For most of us, much like the man above, our perspectives change over time. As I have come to live more and more the Truth of what I am, all around me has changed in correlative fashion. Where it ends only Wisdom knows. Yet Truth shows me that the journey is the purpose and thus validates the end. I'll share a bit of my own journey, so you may discern if there is any parallel to your own.

As I look back, my so-called spiritual quest began in earnest when I took a class teaching the use of "listening prayer," sometime in the early 1990s. I learned that forming Life from a spiritual foundation could open the doors to what inner Truth has to say to me.

I found that dedicating some time each day to devotional preparation, I would then be open to the voice that awaits only my awareness to be heard. All I had to do was faithfully "show up," and this seemingly mysterious source would inform me of spiritual prescience. To say that this was life changing is to render a great understatement. In just a short time, now some twenty years ago, I was afforded the spiritual meaning of surrender and humility, all in one. Learning to get out of my own way provided room for only Highest Good—Wisdom, to surface.

A few years later, as I was sitting at the dining table one evening I heard this inner voice, seemingly out of nowhere, bid me to write some poetry. I had not thought of myself as a poet, at least in the intellectual frame of reference. However, I am poetic when I've allowed the voice within me to speak poetically. In any event, I took out pad and pen and gave myself to the task, only to find out that the intellectual approach was not the way to go. The results were hardly satisfying. Feeling somewhat defeated and misled, I tossed both pad and pen aside and returned to a glass of good red wine and the rest of my meal.

Just as I finished, the inner voice beckoned. "Go to your computer," it directed. "What?" I thought. "That's crazy." "Go to your computer," the voice commanded again. Reluctantly, I gave in and strode to my office desk and opened my faithful Mac laptop. "Put your fingers on the keyboard," came the instructions, "and don't think about anything at all. Just listen." Being obedient, I did just that, waiting patiently for whatever might come. You can believe me when I say I was more than a bit wary of this by now. Despite my wariness, without a moment's notice I heard a word, accompanied by the simple instruction to type it. And so I did. In just a few seconds, out from my fingers onto the screen came a few lines of poetic definition applying to that word. Here are a few examples, each of them coming to me as though defined by some form of inner Wisdom:

flower

a blossom of My smile
on the stem of your heart
from the seed of your soul.

grave

a place bodies go to rest
while their Spirit
dances with Me
through the Universe.

judgmental

the need to have
all be like you
when all are really

already like Me.

limitation

the cramp of the planet
on the soul of the Universe
in the heart of humankind.

This process repeated itself time and again, until, about an hour
or so later, over eighty similar entries had found their way onto
the screen. I was stunned, truly amazed by what had transpired.
All I did was to get out of my own way and listen, and had this
to show for it. Entitled *God's Pocket Dictionary*, the full collection
awaits publication.

A few years later, I attended in Santa Fe a public reading by
Coleman Barks of his latest translation of Rumi's poetry. The
setting was highly spirited, with over 800 persons attending.
Accompanied by a dancer, cellist, and drummer, their collective
talent made for an immensely powerful performance. Everyone
present seemed to glow; the loving energy was that palpable.

The day after the performance I purchased two of Bark's
books for him to autograph at an event hosted by a local
bookstore. As I approached him, there was one man in line in
front of me and three or four women behind. As the man left, I
handed the books to Barks and told him that the first was for a
friend. He asked what my friend did and then wrote a greeting
akin to that in the book. He then looked up and asked me what I
did. Without thinking about it my mouth opened and out came,
"I make love all day." I could feel the hair on the necks of the
women behind me stand on end. And he said, "You dickens
you." "Oh, no," I rejoined, "I don't mean that sexually. What you
and your friends did last night at the theater was to make love
with one another and everyone there. It was a truly loving
testimony." Immediately, I felt the "standing hair" relax in the

5

wake of spiritual translation. Barks said not another word, only handed the second book back to me. I was briefly taken aback by his lack of response, but thanked him and turned and went on my way. "Must be he didn't get it," I remember saying to myself.

Later that morning I called the person who so thoughtfully made tickets available for my friends and me to attend the performance. When I told her of my earlier encounter with Barks, she said, "Jim, you have no idea what you've done. It's no wonder he responded like he did." "Whatever do you mean?" I responded. "Well," she explained, "last night was the first time he brought the new love of his life to a performance, and she was sitting in the front row. More than likely he was completely thrown by the thought that you could have known." Stunned again.

There's more to the story. After a cup of tea to celebrate synchronicity, I felt guided to my laptop, much like the time I was directed to write some poetry. Over the next few weeks, obedience brought glory to a series of poetic references that ended up in a book entitled, *On Making Love*—spiritually, of course. Getting out of my own way was becoming a habit I was beginning to enjoy.

The most recent leg of this journey happened just over five years ago, while I was in the midst of a rather serious relationship. The deeper I let myself be with the relationship, the more my "gut" seemed to argue for my attention. I asked for clarity but didn't get it right away. Thinking I needed a different perspective on what was going on, I decided to give myself some space by taking a trip to visit some friends.

On the way there, I noticed that a red light flashed on my dashboard every time I braked for an oncoming curve in the road. As a matter of course, I knew one of my brake lights must have burned out. Not one for leaving evidence only in the physical realm, I wondered half out loud what the metaphorical meaning must be. Instantly, I heard this: "When you take time to slow down, you'll be enlightened." Talk about admonition! Slow down I did, instantly, both in mind and body. By the time I reached my destination the fullness of awareness had spoken in abundance and clarity.

Over the previous few years I had felt an inner nagging calling me to write, about what, I never really defined for myself. Of course, that should have been my clue: *I* was trying to define it, when I'm not the seat of inspiration. What I learned in that magnificent awakening was that I had been ignoring the inner "pearl of great price," and needed to face that potential in order for the nagging to stop. Facing it full square, I learned that some huge offering was about to appear, and I would need to decide whether I was going to serve the calling or the relationship. Even more to the point, it became clear that one of these two could not be served without great detriment to the other. Giving myself permission to hear the ultimate Truth of the matter, full awareness led me to make myself available for the pearl to surface.

Thus I made myself completely available to the voice I had learned to abide. This sacred relationship had never failed me before, and was fast becoming the sole source of inspiration for my walk on this planet. In less than a week, I heard the command to sit at my laptop yet again. Having no idea whatsoever what was about to open to me, I simply trusted and took myself there, listening and recording obediently. Just over three years later, no less than ten spiritual books had come through me, with this one forming close on the heels of the rest. I use "have come through me" advisedly, for there's no way I could have planned and written that volume through intellect alone. As a former academic, I know what such writing commands, and it is only by getting out of my own way and agreeing to serve as a scribe that these could have manifested as they have.

This may seem like a long way to go to make a point. Yet, here it is. The seemingly bad news about the mystical or a Life of Spirit is that it takes showing up in a dedicated, disciplined way over time. For various reasons, there aren't many willing to give themselves to spiritual Life in this way. Mostly, it takes years, especially if one thinks he needs to be in control of everything that surrounds him. After all, being humble enough to surrender to what we really are instead of staying entrenched in who we've come to believe we are takes not only courage but also a good deal of practice—practice of getting out of our own way. It also takes an inner understanding that it us not inspiration that takes us to the seat of Truth. It is discipline.

The good news is that you come to indelible clarity about spiritual demonstration: inspiration is the form of clear direction waiting for you to show up, so you can become aware of—and express individually—Spirit's authentic renderings. Inspiration speaks only in terms of greatest good, but not just for you. Such gifts are there for more universal purpose.

Don't let the thought of extensive commitment over a long time dissuade you from your inner journey. Given that the embodiment of Wisdom is eternal, this idea of time is but a blink of an eye in the larger view of Life. Just give yourself to this journey and let it serve what it will to you, day by momentous day.

Spiritually, these revelations bring great comfort. Without doubt they have led me to know that there is only one true source that frees me to express what I really am. It's the road less traveled, found only in the voice that speaks in silence, the voice of Wisdom. All the rest is but a mistranslation of Truth.

Join with me, then, in exploring the inner will that waits to be set free. Let us discover our true identity, found only in spiritual freedom. There is only One, after all.

Jim Young

Every happening, great and small,
is a parable whereby God speaks to us,
and the art of life is to get the message.

Malcolm Muggeridge

Chapter One

Preparing the Soil

"Now I will do nothing but listen,
To accrue what I hear into this song."
Walt Whitman

Before spiritual Life can successfully come to awareness, the soil of our soul must be tilled and nourished. Chapter One is the beginning of that process. We'll begin tilling and nourishing our spiritual foundation with some essential understandings about Life, purpose, spirituality, and awareness. In this way we will be fulfilling the scriptural admonishment to "put your hand on the tiller and don't let go," so as to maintain a steady path to enlightenment and fruitage. We would do well to look only inward in each moment of now, and not outwardly, for our true identity.

Aware in a world asleep

I was tempted to introduce this portion differently, using the word "awake," instead of "aware." However, quick discernment of the more superficial meaning of awake gave way to the surer, deeper sense of Life found in the word aware. Simply put, most of us think we're awake when we see the world around us, separate from—and falsely thought to be different from—sleep time. The meaning of awareness speaks to a much deeper understanding of spiritual Life.

Awareness, not unlike intuition, is Wisdom—Truth—coming to light in ways we can realize it for what it is. As used in this book, Wisdom refers to a full and authentic engagement with our inherent godliness, piety and with the inner experiencing of Truth heard when fully aware. Such Wisdom far exceeds surface "knowledge" thought to be true. Many will tell us that Wisdom comes from experience, yet we find the deeper meaning of Wisdom even in children, who come to it out of innocence. And we find it in characters like the one playing the main role in the movie, "Forest Gump," who, for whatever reason, puts nothing in the way of it so it can surface in simple profundity.

To be conscious is to reveal the meaning of one's surroundings and identity. It is to be spiritually sensitive, knowledgeable and enlightened—not from what we are led to believe from those who take meaning from the world of ego—but from what we "just know" is right for us. We experience this feeling of "Truth-speaking" only inwardly. When in communion with what we'll come to witness as Wisdom revealed, we become aware of our only real identity. We become aware of the spiritual evidence that reframes the way we see and express Life. Intuition and insight are that for us, released out of this sacred connection within us. They never let us down as deliverances or "angelic" messages to be lived faithfully.

When spiritually aware we hear a calling in the silence of our hearts. We must be careful to refrain from thinking simplistically that silence refers only to the lack of noise. When we speak of silence spiritually it means we are to silence our own beliefs and opinions, putting aside what we have learned from outer authority. Surrendering our old ways in this fashion is the depth and breadth of humility, giving up our own views entirely for the Truth or Wisdom heard within us. Responding otherwise puts the world on notice that we think we know better than God. In reality, I know nothing of what is best for me; the best I can know is what I desire and even that is colored by outside influence.

Spiritually, Wisdom is that which "knocks on our inner door," the voice that speaks only of our highest good. Silence is the language God speaks—a divine gift, each a "pearl of great price." We are moved to respond as we grasp its full meaning.

Renewed inner meaning quickens the soul and becomes our purpose. Graces abounds, and we ennoble the creation process by faithfully expressing this gift to the Universe. To be otherwise is to be asleep—asleep to the Wisdom that waits only to be heard and brought into being. Awareness, revealed often as intuition, is thus the key that opens the door to the One and only Truth for each of us.

When asleep—when distracted and unaware—we are unable to hear that still, small voice. Asleep in this context refers to being numbed or deadened to inner awareness. It refers to ignorance, devoid of insight and enlightenment. We are rendered asleep primarily through distraction. In the allegory of Adam and Eve we find Adam asleep to divine creation, dreaming that he also creates, a sign that the self-absorbed ways of ego consciousness are major distractions to abiding inner Wisdom. You will recall from Scripture that Master Jesus referred to the sleeping disciples, who, while he traversed the "higher ground of enlightenment," grounded themselves in ignorance by giving credence to fear. In another story, Jesus pointed out that while Mary was paying attention to spiritual discernment and divine consciousness, Martha was essentially asleep to spiritual need through her investment in the distractions of material life. Each of these is an example of a dualistic illusion that most assuredly distracts from spiritual reality.

Falling asleep, living in ignorance of spiritual Truth, is what we strive to overcome. Living in ignorance is what causes us to miss the mark of spiritual Life. It is ignorance—not the sin or some erroneous behavior or thought—from which me must be saved. For when we come to fully appreciate and activate Wisdom through intuition, we no longer miss the mark of spirituality and true Life.

Simply put, there is only one power, not many. One God, not God and... This God is our Highest Self, Wisdom, Truth, and Life, given some familiar names. Once distracted from this spiritual reality, we are asleep—thus unaware of true reality and purpose. In contrast, when aware, we hear Wisdom's voice speak: *God, or Wisdom, is*. Period. Once we are able to declare this as the way for us, we cease to speak or ask of some god external to us. We listen only. And as we listen spiritually, we learn that we've missed our purpose all along. Instead of seeking something or someone to complete us, we're to become aware only of what we already are. This I call "The Inward Way."

The influence of distraction

There are many pragmatic ways of dealing with distraction in an ego-centered world. For example, a few years ago a young friend shared with me that he was smitten with someone he had just met. After just a few weeks, he told me he had decided to severe the relationship. "What happened?" I asked, "I thought from your description that she was the one for you." "Well, it's like when I shaved my head," he responded. Confused, I asked, "You shaved your head because of her?" "No, that's not it," he responded. "A few months ago I was having a crazy time with my hair. I couldn't decide what style I liked, whether or not to use mousse, all that kind of thing. Finally, I decided it was just too much of a distraction, so I shaved my head. It's the same thing that happened with this relationship. No matter what I said to her, she insisted on calling me way too frequently throughout each day. I had my life's work to do, and the calls just became a major distraction from that inner commitment."

Ever since, when distraction has become a major influence in either of our lives, we just say, "shave your head" as the buzzword (pun intended) for the necessary action to be taken. You might adopt that as a simple way of dealing with what distracts you from your spiritual purpose: quite simply, "shave your head." Unnecessary distraction deserves no less drastic, yet simple, solution.

Needless to say, there are many things that distract us from awareness. Many of them are not of our own making. Examples are amply spelled out in the next chapter. Not to be hated or even disliked, distractions just are what they are. Used simply as evidence of what separates us from allowing Wisdom to become conscious, we can immediately shift our direction, restoring our consciousness to that found within our heart of hearts.

Experiencing Life

It is important to distinguish between what we mean by real Life and the dream-like circumstances and conditions we observe around us. The difference is profound, yet quite simple. On one hand, we express our day-to-day existence largely unconsciously, or from the illusory foundation of ego or mass consciousness. These make for waking dreams, symbolic representations of some material desire or unconscious manifestation. Once believed, these desires become our reality—or so we think.

We might well try looking at what we believe material life to be by first understanding the nature of our sleeping dreams. Essentially, they are a symbolic representation reflecting some aspect of our current state of consciousness. Quite often they are a reflection of our hidden so-called "treasures," those false images that need to surface in order to be finally swept aside. Read symbolically, we can discern the path for empowering a helpful change in outlook. Indeed, each dream is a gift when seen that way.

Why not, then, see our waking life in the same light? Learning to see outward appearance as the symbolic representation of our current level of spiritual consciousness can enlighten us to the deeper meaning events and circumstances have for us. They also afford us greater comprehension of what is happening within us. In this way, no matter what we find outside ourselves, on the deeper level of awareness it also is a gift that informs us spiritually. Each external event is like a mirror reflecting our consciousness back to us, so we can discern inner Life more easily. As we practice looking at each external event and circumstance as a reflection of our inner state, we learn about the depth of spiritual connectedness with each other and the world around us. We also learn that our external world is much less threatening when we are able to look at it from a more detached viewpoint.

A quick example might be helpful here. Let's say that you are disturbed by some element of another's behavior. You are troubled by what appears to be the manipulative ways he uses to gain your favor. In the context of outer appearance informing inner spiritual perspective, the manipulative behavior says only that he has a need to manipulate for some reason. The distraction is feeling the need to know why he is doing it, or simply feeling the need to stop it. Perhaps he feels powerless to gain your approval unless he does manipulate. Neither the reason nor his life history in this regard really matters. What matters is that his behavior got your attention. Spiritually speaking, that's the only thing that does matter in this exchange.

The key that it is a gift to you is the strong feeling you have about feeling manipulated. Such a strong reaction is a sure sign that you have failed to see that you, too, on some level, manipulate, or allow yourself to be manipulated. At the deepest, spiritual level, you might ask yourself a question something like this: "How is it that I manipulate my life to keep from listening to the One and only Truth that resides in me?" Or, to keep it simple, "I wonder what this feeling is trying to tell me about myself?" Exercising "I wonder" is an insightful and powerful way to reach inner meaning. Taken to the only place where the query can be truthfully answered, to the still small voice of Wisdom, the answer will come to consciousness with indelible clarity.

Likewise, if you allow yourself to wallow in the other's manipulative ways without examining your reactions, you will remain a victim of your own behavior that keeps you in darkness. Interestingly, merely acknowledging the strong feelings alone—without unnecessary intellectual pursuit— usually frees up the inner spaciousness for the answer to reach the surface. Just listening to what the feeling is telling us is often enough to free the nature of its cause. The sudden awareness found in intuition or insight enlightens us, while ignoring it or judging someone else for his behavior eliminates that potential.

What someone else does says something only about them, not about us. Their words only trouble us when we give them the power of our attention. We can still the manipulative behavior as long as we understand that their behavior or projection is theirs, and not at all about us. Then we can laugh at the thought that we gave it power and resume our relationship with them using inner guidance. Otherwise, we are giving power to the wrong teacher. Giving no power to outside appearance is the way, listening only to the Truth of the matter, found only in the Wisdom heard in silence.

On a strictly spiritual basis, Life suggests that inner Wisdom is the Truth we are to express. Aristotle called this dimension of consciousness "First Cause." What he meant by this designation is that awareness of Wisdom is the only *real* Cause. Therefore, it is always first—not serially, mind you—but the first and *only*. This is such an important Truth to fully comprehend. Wisdom truly heard is what instills and initiates all authentic demonstration. Wisdom found in inspiration is that which *parents* **all** expressions of its awareness. In the vernacular of "old world" theology, inspiration, Wisdom, is the Father of all demonstration, but that is its literal meaning; we are speaking spiritually here, where Father means "to parent," or bring to Life.

Life is not experience itself. Such a designation of experience falsely renders us as victims of outward appearance. Given a spiritual context, experience is framed by the nature of consciousness we are reflecting each moment. In this way, experience becomes an active verb instead of some complacent noun. We are quickened to the core by the difference. In this spiritual state, we come to see that appearance is not Truth. We comprehend that only Wisdom brought to spiritual awareness is Truth speaking to us.

Any judgmental label I place on some outward appearance renders my experience of it. I make it something it is not. Any physical appearance, any event or circumstance, is simply what it is, and needs no label at all. It is the labeling that causes attachment of judgmental feeling to it—what gives the imaginary power to it. And what creates duality as something real. Nothing, in and of itself, has power. Only attaching the meaning it has for us gives power to it. Labeling something good or bad, for example, gives it power or meaning it simply does not have. Sometimes we give meaning that feels emotional, at other times it is intellectual, and at still other times, spiritual. I just love this definition I once heard of "name," as in "naming something:" Name is a label, when stripped away, that let's you see all as Me. "Me," of course, refers to divine essence individualized infinitely. It is our conscious awareness of God, Wisdom, expressed as each of us. What is simply is, regardless of appearance. Perhaps a brief story will help here.

A friend once told me of her time in India, where she studied in an ashram. Over the door to the ashram was a sign: "Is-ness is our business." This was intended to admonish the followers that any form of labeling or judgment attached to simple Is-ness was not part of why they were there. Long story short, the guru they studied under died suddenly one night, throwing the followers into disarray. As they entered the ashram the next morning, the followers were greeted with a new sign: "Is-ness as usual." In the words of Shakespeare, nothing is either right or wrong, only thinking makes it so. The same is true with labeling or making unfound judgments out of dualistic limitation. Life just is what it is, period. According to the Master Jesus, we are to give it no more thought or concern to Life than that.

A keener sense of spiritual accountability comes from being

more aware of the consequences of our actions. From this we learn that our lives are essentially about demonstrating spiritual awareness. In this physical form, we are able to see the effects of how we express our current level of consciousness. Many of us are threatened by the idea of personal accountability. We do not like to think we have created what we see around us. However, accountability is not a judgmental term. It only connotes a confirmation of action taken or experience defined. It is the demonstration or proof one can use to assess behavior, or action alongside results. We can then use our discernment to modify our demonstrations to expressions of divine consciousness only. Each moment welcomes an opportunity for doing so. One day we will come to free ourselves from enough limitations to see beyond the veil of illusion. We will move past the false beliefs and opinions that have reserved our place in the illusory chaotic, ego-centered world. Instead, we will come to see and feel the connection with something larger than ourselves: the essence of Being, by whatever name one wants to put on it. The rest of what we see outside us is just a dream we make up as we go along.

In this regard, divine essence or Wisdom cannot really be described. It must be experienced in order for it to be real for us. Thus experiencing becomes the definition. No matter what appears before us, then, it is how we experience that idea, and not the element itself, that defines spiritual reality. We resonate with the Truth we find there—and then apply or express it as Life. Contrary to popular belief, there is no other way to the Truth of the matter, at least not spiritually.

Eventually we come to comprehend that, as humans, we are not the creator at all. The actual creator of Life is the Wisdom that inspires us to act. It is this spiritual voice that parents its demonstration. We are simply the mechanism through which demonstration unfolds. This is not to minimize our part in it. Without us, creations lay fallow in the field of unrealized potential.

Demonstration is initiated by inspiration, the voice of

intuition or insight heard as the still, small voice within us. Heard as the highest good, we activate or energize this Wisdom with the voice of enthusiasm for its completion. When complete, we get to assess the validity of how we have demonstrated it. Either it has been faithfully rendered as the highest form of Love or it has been erroneously formed out of fear.

Deeper meaning

It is important to reinforce that this Life is about the spiritual world, although the physical or material could be highly influenced or affected by the spiritual. It is in the realm of divine inspiration that spiritual direction is revealed with clarity.

Spiritual Life or inspiration cannot be proven through physics, by material, or with the physical body, and certainly not with beliefs or opinions. This is what is meant by the term metaphysics: spiritual experience is beyond physical evidence. Further to the point, metaphysics speaks to what it is that orders our lives on a day-to-day basis. What we are talking about is the state of spiritual or divine consciousness, about the sacred ideas held in Wisdom, and not intellectual pursuit. Intellectual pursuit without spiritual comprehension is like an egg with no yolk, devoid of any real substance—Life without Soul.

This is why we sometimes feel we are *in* this world but not *of* it. Somehow, we feel disjointed or out of place, in disarray. That is because, lodged in a physical mentality, we *are* out of place and disjointed, and in disarray. For the most part, we have forgotten yet again that Life is really spiritual. Instead, we have inserted a collective belief that renders both the spiritual and physical as equals and real. Thus, we hold ourselves in a pattern encumbered with illusions tied to duality, while our inner voice beckons with the Truth of Oneness.

We often confuse outer appearances with True reality. Collective consciousness harnessed and impressed over centuries has led us to believe these illusions are real, even spiritually. As we engage with a false sense of ego consciousness, we require evidence gathered from our five senses as the means of validating reality. Let us imagine that we can see only with our eyes and hear only with our ears. One could argue that it is the optic and auditory nerves that make sight and sound possible, but bear with me for just a moment. If true as a spiritual proposition, why then did the Master Jesus say we have eyes but do not see, and ears but do not hear? On the surface of it, much like the Pharisees dealt with spirituality, Jesus' words must have sounded absurd. As physical references, they *are* absurd. But spirituality does not deal with the physical world. It deals with experiencing and demonstrating Wisdom, surfacing as spiritual Truth.

Jesus admonished us to look at God and Life spiritually, not physically. Jesus' words, just as the Word we attribute to God, speak as metaphor, as poetic reflections of deeper meaning. "Seeing" refers to intuition or insight, and "hearing" refers to deeper meaning or spiritual comprehension. To comprehend is to conceive or grasp the *fullness* of meaning, in this case, the Truth heard deep within us. Seeing and hearing are not about surface meaning, literality, linearity, or physicality. It's about experiencing Wisdom at its depths and resonating with it as Truth for us. There is no resonant connection that can reconcile spiritual meaning physically. Spiritually, the physical is deader than a doornail. No matter what physical nail we are hitting, it is only by experiencing inner resonance that we understand with certainty we have come to the Truth of any matter. *This* is conscious awareness.

Life as purpose fulfilled

Spiritually speaking, our purpose is to become aware of and express the perfection of the Wisdom we are. A belief in a self apart from God or Wisdom is the height of dualism, because if conscious awareness of inner Wisdom is omniscient, omnipotent, omnipresent, and ever active, where is there room for anything else to be found? Nowhere. There is no God, no Wisdom and everything else. Spiritually, there only is the awareness of this Truth. All else we think is real is only an illusion thought to be real.

The minute we give credence or power to outer appearance or belief and opinion we separate ourselves from the One, divine consciousness. We will have succumbed to the voice of outer authority, when the only real Authority resides within, in the form of Wisdom. Erroneously, duality will have been validated as real, when it is not. Denial of this Truth represents a belief in a self apart from God, Wisdom. Such a sense of separation is the height of vanity. As the height of ill-found dualism, Shakespeare would call it the vanity of vanities.

Try envisioning the One individualized as us this way. Picture a large piece of exquisitely fashioned crystal. Drop it to the floor and see it shatter to pieces. What remains is still crystal, is it not? The thing that is different is the shape of each individual fragment, but the substance remains the same. This is what it means to be Oneness individualized.

On a day-to-day basis, we are our current consciousness expressed. To be sure, what we see outside us is merely an out picturing or manifestation of our consciousness at the moment. If we are expressing the falsity of ego-consciousness, then outer circumstances and events are likely to be in disarray and erratically formed. Becoming more open to the conscious awareness of the Wisdom residing within, we make considerable shifts that overcome past perceptions and deceptions tied to the illusions of ego consciousness.

Our lives reflect this new depth of meaning. We come to see that so-called physical body is not physical at all, but a body of current conscious awareness. This is the body Master Jesus spoke of when he told us we would be taking our body with us when we drop the physical one. Whatever constitutes our level of consciousness at our moment of physical passing is what goes with us as our ascended body, albeit an esoteric one.

With this in mind, it is clear that I am not Jim, but the idea of Jim—*my current* idea of Jim, expressed outwardly. We are all similar in this regard, so it behooves us to become more consciously aware of our engagement with Wisdom, so we can express *that* faithfully instead. I often wonder what a more conscious awareness of inner Wisdom would say about the idea of Jim I currently hold. Only my full spiritual awareness will bypass or supersede the plethora of limitations I have placed on such an idea.

The power of listening

A metaphysical society which I helped form has put spiritual discernment and the process for exercising it essentially this way:

"We gather as seekers of inner meaning, wisdom and the nature of unseen realities. None of us has a complete picture of our own being or the greater existence of consciousness, so we come together from our myriad paths seeking to add to a greater comprehension, while sharing in the inner knowledge and experience of others on a similar journey. In this we honor and celebrate our differences and the process of spiritual inquiry. We are not a group consisting of people seeking therapy; we are not a debating society; neither are we a platform for personal, economic, or political agendas.

Thus our only imperative is to listen while deeper meaning seeks our awareness."

Such treatment of Life requires a level of listening that is akin to hearing and celebrating the beauty punctuated by the silence heard among falling snowflakes. While meditating, it is not in the images that cross our minds that we find Wisdom. We find Wisdom by patiently acknowledging the spaces between the images—and by experiencing the conscious awareness we find there.

Spiritual discernment is not found in one's beliefs or opinions, for they limit us in significant ways. Beliefs and opinions distract from purposeful spiritual experience. This is akin to looking for the Big Dipper at high noon; it will not be visible then. The distractions are just too great and the conditions not just right. The same is true when we look for the spiritual Truth in the world of opinion and belief. We become distracted by the immense layer of errors held in place by the demands of so-called physical proof. We look endlessly in the material realm for validation of false claims. So duality surfaces again and again as a false idol. Yet again, we need to "shave our head" of distraction from spiritual reality.

Sometimes we hear inner Truth or conscious awareness expressed as an "aha" moment. It also comes to us through intuition or as a sudden insight. Every so often it strikes like a bolt of lightning, enlightening us to some new awareness. Also, by practicing spiritual inquiry, that is, by asking inwardly if a certain path is right for us just now, we can learn to hear a spiritual answer that is to be revered. We are spiritually uplifted by the gifts we find there, and are transformed in the process.

Contrary to common belief and practice, conscious awareness also comes to us when we stop thinking about a question that troubles us and let Life simply bring awareness to us sometime during the day, or as a bump in the night. It is impossible for us to receive the gifts that await us when we are grinding away trying to dig them out for ourselves. Indeed, we are far better off following Jesus' admonition to "give it no thought." Silencing our erroneous beliefs and opinions, instead of giving them thought, allows the language of Wisdom to surface. It is about letting Wisdom have its way with us. And it is only there where Truth is found.

Sometimes dualistic references get in our way of real meaning, and we often explain them away by saying it is only a matter of semantics. For example, some use the word "Mind" to describe divine consciousness. From the seat of ego consciousness, however, Mind and the physical brain are often erroneously interchanged. Spiritually, we are not speaking about the intellect or brainpower, or some physical part of us. When aware, darkness or ignorance is dispelled by enlightenment. Enlightenment only appears when we understand that this is not a dualistic world we live in. That difference cannot be explained by semantics.

In order to keep the discussion focused on the spiritual and away from duality I suggest we substitute Wisdom," or even simply "conscious awareness," for the word "God" and all its synonyms. Until we are solidly grounded in spiritual comprehension, it is simply too easy to slide back into duality by holding to a view of God as some entity aside from us. This only recreates God as man's false image and is all too easily believed. It can also take us back to our religious upbringing, for better or worse. Conscious awareness, Wisdom or inspiration conveys spiritual meaning, the deeper meaning or consciousness that is pure and perfect spiritual essence. Spiritual meaning emphasizes that Wisdom is the deepest and only spiritual level of consciousness. It also emphasizes the difference between the consciousness of God and the falsely held beliefs and opinions we obtain from the illusory world of ego. The ego and mass or collective consciousness express only illusion, a waking dream, a false world of duality, and not spiritual reality at all.

Spiritual discernment

I come at spiritual discernment with one basic premise: daily activity and appearances, like art, are not here to answer questions; they are here to ask them. Such outer signs act as mirrors to direct our eyes, our spiritual vision as it were, to real answers. Spiritual consciousness awareness becomes clearer and clearer to us as our ability to hear the still, small voice of Wisdom within improves.

No less than Ralph Waldo Emerson validates this claim in his treatise, "Self-reliance:"

"A foolish consistency is the hobgoblin of little minds, adored by little statesmen, philosophers and divines. With consistency a great soul has simply nothing to do...Speak what you think now in hard words and tomorrow speak what tomorrow thinks in hard words again, though it contradicts everything you said today...

'Ah, so you shall be sure to be misunderstood'... Is it so bad then to be misunderstood? Pythagorus was misunderstood, and Socrates, and Jesus, and Luther, and Newton, and every pure and wise spirit that ever took flesh. To be great is to be misunderstood." (p. 95)

"A foolish consistency," reflects those self-limiting beliefs or opinions that entwine us in the never-ending web of ego-centered restriction and imaginational bias. We become rigid in these perceptions. We fight to the death for them. We make our beliefs and opinions, along with outer appearances, sound like the Truth when they are not. Spiritually, this obviates going within for the only real source of Truth on any matter. Nor do we question any of the mythology that has held our dysfunctional world of duality in place. Indeed, a foolish consistency is the mischievous imp that leads us astray from the conscious awareness of inner Wisdom.

"Thinking," as Emerson uses the term, is not about intellectual pursuit so often applied by literalists. It is about the awareness of Wisdom we find by listening for the still, small voice and coming to deeper meaning. The Truth of which Emerson speaks he calls "intuitions." Intuition releases real meaning: Truth heard in silence, the language Wisdom speaks.

Emerson calls this perpetual spiritual sourcing from intuition self-reliance. I call it Self-reliance in order to highlight the Self as our spiritual and most natural state of being.

The real point of questions is neither the importance of answers nor even the process used to obtain them. Each question is simply a reminder to go into our heart, to the source of the only truthful answer to any of them. This is the only real source because the only real question, like the only real Life, is spiritual in nature. Otherwise, we find ourselves once again in the lap of duality. This great source of Truth is what Jesus called "the Kingdom within." We arrive at the Kingdom through awareness. When practiced faithfully, we are rewarded with the only genuine pathway for each of us. Indeed, each answer is a "pearl of great price." When we fail to grasp and express each pearl as it is revealed to us, we do so at our spiritual peril.

What is the vehicle that guides you through Life?

There is a story that made the rounds on Internet recently. I have used it widely in presentations about spiritual discernment. As the story unfolds, we find the global evangelist Rev. Billy Graham talking with his chauffeur. "You know," said Rev. Graham, "I've always wanted to know what it's like to drive one of these limousines, but I've only ridden in the back of one all these years." "Oh, no, Rev. Graham, I couldn't let you do that. You're the important one here." "No, that isn't so, we're all important. Besides, I'd like to satisfy my curiosity. Please indulge me this one time." The chauffeur thought it over and reluctantly turned the wheel over to Rev. Graham, resigning himself to the back seat as instructed.

Unaccustomed as he was to driving such a large, powerful vehicle, Rev. Graham quickly exceeded the speed limit after entering the freeway. Almost immediately a policeman pulled him over and asked for his driver's license and registration. Embarrassed, Rev. Graham fumbled for them, declaring that he normally didn't drive, so didn't have them right at hand. Now, fully recognizing Rev. Graham, the officer told him he had to check something at headquarters and would return momentarily.

Once on the intercom, the officer asked the desk sergeant if they still had the policy of giving preferential treatment to special persons. "Why, yes," answered the sergeant, "Why do you ask?" "Well," the officer responded, "I've just stopped a really important person, and I want to be sure to do the right thing." "Well, who is it, the governor?" "No," answered the officer, "more important than that." "The President?" the desk sergeant asked again. "No, even more important than that," the officer responded. "How can that be? Who could be more important than the President?" the other asked incredulously. "Well," responded the field officer, "to be honest, it must be Jesus, because Rev. Billy Graham is his chauffeur."

Not only does this story tickle our fancy; it goes to the core of divine consciousness by raising some very important questions. Metaphorically speaking, an automobile represents the vehicle of consciousness that transports us through Life. From time to time we erroneously think Life is governed or driven by some outside force, when spiritual reality is governed by the power of conscious awareness. We thus make false assumptions that overvalue one by forgetting or ignoring the other. Questions arise, then: Are we allowing ourselves to be transported through Life by the illusions of duality or the Truth found in Self-reliance? What is really driving us? Who or what is being transported? What pattern of governance are we using to shape Life? Are we deferring to some outer authority from which we seek answers, as depicted by the storied version of Rev. Graham? Or are we abiding in the Truth found in the still small voice that validates our only real identity— the Christ or Wisdom that spoke through Jesus, and thus which also speaks through us? Once we come to see that the Truth found in Wisdom has only one source, illusions of dualism cease to exist as viable alternatives.

The need for spiritual principles

By discovering some spiritual principles to guide us, we can practice expressing Life consonant with them. We can transform our lives through the essence of Spirit instead of wallowing in the disarray of a world that sees itself apart from God.

At the core of such principles is the necessity to stay aware of our inherent Wisdom and be faithful only to that. The principles illumined in the following chapters will help establish a pattern for doing so, for more regularly arriving at conscious awareness.

For this deeper comprehension of our spirituality—awareness—I have coined the word gnowing. Some would call this a rather esoteric or affected utterance, but I prefer to think of it simply as a way of expressing the Truth of the matter. As a practical matter, both "gnow" and "know" begin with a silent letter. I like "gnow" better because it speaks to the meaning of gnosis: the deeper comprehension found only in the depths of our hearts. The Gnostics often spoke of "real" Truth or the voice of Wisdom this way, in contrast to the superficial knowledge found so frequently by using the intellect or literal, rational treatment alone. Thus knowing turns into gnowing—if for no other purpose than for spiritual clarity and emphasis. Divine consciousness is the gnowing or conscious awareness of spiritual Truth found in Wisdom, while knowing is most often only an intellectual or literal rendering that, at best, can only point the direction to Truth. This is not to demean intellect, only to acknowledge it for what it is instead of giving it some magic power it does not have.

The terms ego and collective or mass consciousness are used to refer to the erroneous belief in the idea of a life separate from God. Neither they nor what they deliver to us are real; we only think that to be true. When we are able to discern this illusion through awareness, we cease experiencing duality. We awaken from the dream and experience communion with all that is.

If we continue expressing ourselves from the false imagery of ego or mass consciousness, eventually we will come to see this as too high a price to pay for nothing but empty promises. Spiritual perception sharpens through the acknowledgement of infinite spiritual potential. As our views of Life are reformed, reframed, and enlightened we succumb to a Life grounded only by the voice of Wisdom heard in silence. Here and now we find the spiritual reality that is to be lived and celebrated as our only real identity.

There are those who would have us attempt to become perfect at replicating some religious dictates. We are led to believe we must earn our way into some illusory heaven. Let this false premise or idol fall by the wayside. Living through spiritual awareness is heaven on earth, and we already have all we need to maintain our place there. Awareness of the Truth Wisdom speaks is the place and the only substance, all as One.

The principles we'll soon see form real gnowing, the deeper meaning established as we investigate the foundation for living spiritually. Before we get into them, however, I will take you on a brief journey to the "land of nod." "The land of nod" is the territory attributable to concepts, beliefs and opinions that have put us asleep spiritually. They have rendered us "dead to the world," and "dead on our feet," and to the Life of Spirit, and thus to the way of conscious awareness. It is this kind of sleep and death from which Jesus awakened others. And now, the way for fulfilling his promise to us is found.

Chapter Two

How Has Life Gotten Me Here?

"Creatures of stillness
...quiet in themselves,
...from simply listening
...you built a temple inside their hearing."
Rainer Maria Rilke

The title of this chapter suggests perhaps the most frequently expressed frustration of our times. It also implies that we are victims of Life. How did I get to this? How is it that my life has taken so many crazy turns? Why are my relationships, both at work and in general, so dysfunctional? I am sure you can suggest more than these, and even more personally. The point is not the questions so much; it is the cause that makes the questions pertinent. The questions are pertinent largely because we approach Life unconsciously. At the very least, we are forgetful of our real essence.

I will refrain from getting into being unconscious for now, for that is the focus of the first principle, which follows in the next chapter. What I will touch on instead could help explain how we got ourselves into this so-called mess in the first place.

Right at the beginning I want to dispel the mistaken notion that we have to undo all of our past—every discomforting incident and emotional trauma—before we can live a fruitful, happily fulfilled Life *now*. Some psychological models would have us believe that we do. To be sure, some of us can benefit from a wise counselor who can help us see what pattern is keeping us from moving forward from the foundation of our own inner Authority. Before we can realize this fully for ourselves, however, seeing that we are not all alone on the spiritual journey can relieve us of those deep inner feelings of loneliness. Indeed we have plenty of company as we traverse this imaginary panoply of disarray.

The most important thing for us to fully understand is that there is really nothing to "get over." There is no thing to do away with in order to reach spiritual fulfillment. Any and all of those memories and impressions that distract us from living only in the depths of our hearts right now are from the past. They are no longer real, much like the images in a dream from yesteryear. So, if they are no longer real, what is to give up? Nothing—no thing at all!

Here is a hint about this that may surprise you. Years ago, during a special "listening prayer" session, I was clearly admonished to refrain from entertaining *any and all* memories. Not just bad ones or "nightmares," mind you, but even the good ones. This may sound strange, especially since the good ones often take us to some warm and fuzzy place, or are at least entertaining. That is precisely the point: they take us somewhere else, generally to some emotional feeling—and away from Being in the present moment.

Further to the point, even labeling memories as good or bad locks them in emotionally. The same is true for sad and pleasant memories alike, when instead each just *is*, no labels attached. Each take us elsewhere, and that elsewhere loads us with some emotional reaction which, in return, releases emotional "chemistry" associated with that memory in every cell of our body. It is akin to rehearsing any kind of event to which we have an emotional attachment, like a relational break-up, death of a loved one, moving into a new neighborhood, or leaving one's employment—even for an exciting new job. Every time we rehearse any of these attachments, the body responds by releasing the chemicals associated with the feelings held, and both the chemicals and feelings become trapped—for good or ill.

And once trapped, there is an occasional calling by inner Source to be set free. If we fail to respond properly, that failure restarts the emotional cycle through rehearsal again. Talk about being stuck in the past!

The point to be made is this: just as the Master Jesus told us long ago, "Give it no thought." This means that we should not "go there," except, perhaps, to acknowledge the memory briefly. However, acknowledging it does not mean we should entertain it, or give it some power or strength it does not have by itself. Each memory has only the power or strength of feeling we give it, and that power is generated by how we think and feel about it. So, if you do not like how you feel, change your thought first; then your feeling will be easier to lighten. Better yet, do not think at all; simply listen to what the memory is telling you, and let Wisdom take over. More than likely it will tell you that you are still rehearsing some associated feeling that needs letting go.

The admonition to stop, look, and listen is a good one here. Stop to acknowledge the memory. Look briefly at it so you can recognize it for what it is. And "listen" for the feeling. Then let go of it, immediately, before you reattach to it or label it emotionally. Then you can get on with living more and more completely in the now, listening for and acknowledging only the inner voice that speaks in—and as—the present, the gift Life is.

Let this process be the training ground for all of Life, for every distraction. What is the pearl here? The real pearl is that none of our past has any real influence on us unless we allow influence. Just forgive it all, give all of it up, no matter what the distraction, and get on with real Life.

Spiritual fulfillment is stymied by vacillating between the illusions of ego consciousness or duality and the Truth of spiritual consciousness. Generally, we stay mired in confusion, the ego's way of maintaining control through fear and guilt. Living in the illusions of ego consciousness is much like an old movie revival: the script remains essentially the same, with only the actors changing. Based in ego consciousness the story line is one of endless physical and mental disarray, stress, frequent disappointment, and feelings of an existence lacking purpose and fulfillment. And we rehearse the story line over and over again, until we can finally hear the inner call telling us that the fictitious play needs to finish its run.

Spiritually, changing the script requires the understanding that the old one consists of memories continually repeated. By rehearsing these memories over and over we make mythology real. Now we put the old script away, along with all the other illusions, never to return. By doing so we are freed to activate the actual Truth, found only within, in each moment of now. In this way we become the storywriter, producer, and director of our very own spiritual script. Life becomes so much better in the process. Actually, the process of spiritual unfoldment *is* Life.

Using a brief sports metaphor, changing our spiritual perspective on Life is akin to asking a golf professional to improve your game. A good teacher will not undo what he sees as wrong, even so much as draw attention to it. Instead, he establishes a pattern for developing a new habit to replace the old, and encourages you to practice frequently until it becomes second nature. Funny thing is, as you begin to realize what's happening to your swing, insight and enlightenment bring forth the rightness of it for you. From then on it becomes a focus only on listening within for that same experience of rightness, and forgetting about giving the swing any more thought. We set aside the old way by giving our lives fully to the new. In living spiritually, the same kind of diligence is required: experiencing—and demonstrating only—the conscious awareness of Wisdom delivered, as we acknowledge, "Here I am, Lord. Speak and I will listen." And we hear in response, "Be still, and gnow I am God."

Taking a few moments to review some of the common elements that appear to have cemented themselves in a realm of duality can be helpful in this regard. You will soon see that the feelings of pain and separation are the central pilings that undergird ego consciousness. Those very keys help define our place in that fictitious realm.

In large part, it is precisely because we do have so much company that we stay trapped in the belief of ego consciousness. The weight of the false image of collective consciousness—and thus duality—is that heavy, that compelling. Or so it seems. However, this is so only in the realm of ego consciousness. When you see the futility of rendering your place in this realm from a more holistic view, you will finally have reached the point of declaring "this is enough"! You come to the realization that you want something that is far more nourishing and fulfilling than illusory or dream imagery. It is then—and hopefully that moment is now—that you will decide to manifest Life from an entirely different point of view.

Becoming familiar with these distractions helps us to begin anew. We repent or reform—the real meaning of being "born again." In this case being "born again" takes on the meaning of living by a new, completely different, set of values. From a completely different foundation of Life's meaning and purpose, we are propelled from the demeaning ways of ego consciousness into the lap of spiritual Truth. We then live moment by moment guided faithfully only toward our highest good. We will be fed continually by the bearings of the Christ, the inner voice of Wisdom, unleashed by the activation of conscious awareness we hold in common.

Let us now get a taste of those things that seemingly force their way into our lives from a foundation of ego consciousness. Do your best to keep from intellectually and emotionally attaching yourself to them. You will know you are detached from them when you no longer feel troubled by them. It is attachment that holds them dear, and it is by simple acknowledgement that you let them go. Such detachment is like watching the space between thoughts instead of holding onto the thoughts themselves.

For example, if troubled by thinking fearful thoughts about your children being out late at night, how do you feel when you let go of the fearful thought? I suspect you will find that fear is not real and you worried for nothing at all. Worry and fret are fear-filled forms of thinking. This gives credence to Jesus' admonition that we cannot improve our lives one cubit by thinking.

Truth emanates from the stillness, while attachment infuses thoughts and feelings with disarray and tension. By exercising detachment from our thoughts and feelings, we will forgive them and release them into the ethers. With that letting go, we allow ourselves to also forget, and release our old ways. In this one major shift the meaning of "forgive and forget" is rendered complete in its spiritual correctness. We can forget that we thought opinions and beliefs to be helpful instead of spiritually limiting, relieving ourselves of any self-judgment along the way. We can now safely give them up completely.

In case you do not fully understand detachment, let us instead use the idea of "taking something seriously" that has little if any real meaning for us. It is said that we entered the illusory world of duality when we took the idea of a life separate from divine consciousness seriously. The idea of a self apart from God is something to be laughed at. It is absurd to take the height of vanity seriously. When we take ourselves too seriously, we are so self-absorbed, so attached to our personal view of self that we give meaning to the actions of others that was never intended, and the Truth of the matter escapes us.

One last admonition: as you saw earlier, everything we see outside us is a physical manifestation mirroring what is going on within us on the spiritual plane. If you want to see how cluttered your ideas about Life are, for example, just look inside your car. Is it cluttered and disheveled, or clean and free of debris? Our automobile is a metaphor for what array of beliefs or understandings is carrying or transporting us through life. If we are in an inner state of disarray, it is likely some aspect of our outer condition will broadcast that to us. Are any of your closets cluttered to the hilt? Is your study heaped with collections of things that have absolutely no bearing on your current life style? These are sure signs that it is time for an internal—and external—housecleaning. There is no room at the inn for the new guests spiritual consciousness has in store for you. They need space in which to flow and form, free from outside distraction.

As we head into this list of seemingly important renderings from outside us, then, let us keep in mind that not only are they physical manifestations, they are also reflections of the current condition of our soul. I will point that out along the way, so you can see for yourself how you can reframe your spiritual Life.

In the beginning

If one were stuck in ego consciousness it would be easy to see that there are many influences on how we have come to think of ourselves. One of the earliest is the strong influence our parents and other family members had on us when we were but a fetus in our mother's womb. From the point of view of ego consciousness and duality, the energy communicated in the environment surrounding us in that period of our lives had a direct impact on how we entered this world.

If any of those we might call "family" had a negative attitude toward us as a potential child, we would have picked that up. The same is true with positive energy or consciousness about such matters. As a fetus, and no less so as a mere child, we are like wet cement: all that falls on us makes some kind of impression. Everything that falls on us strikes our energetic field, our current level of conscious awareness, and begins to form our belief system. These images are what thread the loom upon which we come to weave our existence on this plane. They come to color and decorate our world, for better or for worse. Mostly, the images litter Life's landscape with the imagery of ego consciousness. On one level or another, we take on the imagery of "them and me," and thus duality is there to greet us as we come out into the open.

Beliefs and opinions found in ego consciousness affect the cellular level in ways that are strong and compelling. They remain so until we can restore the remembrance of our own divinity in their stead. Focusing on awareness alerts us to, and erases the scales of, such burnt offerings, much like a self-cleaning oven does. Here we find the meaning of Apostle Paul's reference that "when a child we thought as a child, but now we are adults and can instead think that way." When we are spiritually immature, no matter what our age, we take things personally and create separation out of them—a sure sign of duality. When spiritually mature, however, we take nothing personally, gnowing that we are at One with Wisdom heard. It's just that some of us have forgotten that, even if only for the moment.

We bring these energetic images into the world and they color how we see Life. We might even have come to see that how our family conducted its daily affairs must have been the right or only way to do so. After all, if it weren't right, why would it have been happening this way? The same can be said especially about how our parents related. As neophytes among gods, in the world of relationship we could well take their model as one to be replicated. And replicate it we often do. It is such erroneous patterns that carry us forward as if they are the Truth, but they are not really that. We only imagine them to be.

For instance, the perception, "Mom married Dad, so this is the kind of person that I, too, should marry," has many of us wedded to persons essentially like our father or mother. Such decisions might be okay for us, but usually they only carry the memory of the past forward. For some, the pattern is broken when they feel moved to meet real needs rather than serving the childhood mythology.

Here is a personal example. I recall with indelible clarity an intimate conversation I had with a dear friend who claimed she was having difficulty with her companion. When asked what was troubling her about him, in a voice much like a child's she declared with considerable consternation: "He's not there for me, just like Daddy wasn't there for me." We examined her proclamation further and discovered that not only was he not there for her, but he had also served as a mirror for her to discover that she had not been there for him. Even more importantly, using Byron Katie's work from *Loving What Is*, in turning around her view of it she discovered that she had not been there for herself. Indeed, by using the drama we have written for ourselves as a mirror for the condition of our spiritual vision, we can find much that can be shifted for the better. The lesson is to see our external life as not separate from our internal Life, because they clearly mirror each other. We construct these outward manifestations so we can reflect on them as an inward sign to be dealt with.

An insightful way to comprehend this is to envision your image in a mirror. Envision an image of someone next to you in the mirror, smudging your image in the mirror with layers of mud, mischaracterizing your image. Once you understand that the smudging is only what someone is doing to that reflection or image of you in his consciousness—and not actually you—you are freed from any suffering you might otherwise feel.

After all, you are not merely someone else's image of you, you are for real; a spiritual entity demonstrated individually. It is only when we see ourselves as a reflection of someone else's view of us that we take it personally. When we hold fast to the Truth of our Being instead, such generalizations and judgments fall aside out of their own nothingness. They, like the mud, are rinsed away by the waters of spiritual consciousness.

It is this distance between illusion and spiritual reality that results in suffering. When living a lie instead of Truth, we suffer. We suffer a sense of loss, feelings of desertion or abandonment. The feelings seem real, when their real purpose is to point us to some inner issue we are having with our spiritual relationship, how we are relating to spiritual consciousness. If we feel abandoned, spiritually it could well mean we are somehow abandoning spiritual awareness in favor of outside authority. We suffer until we reunite with the One and only, the inner voice that holds only our highest good for us. Then the longing founded in disparity is released without penalty or event. We are freed as we reunite, free to be what we really are, instead of what we have come to falsely believe about ourselves. In this freedom found in awareness, suffering ceases to exist.

The same would apply to the suffering we feel when believing in lack. We suffer as we work ourselves to the bone to accumulate more personal, material worth, and so we can feel "good enough." Momentarily, we do feel better about ourselves, and the temporary feeling of lack seems to disappear. Rest assured that this feeling of lack is sure to reappear, time and again, until we fathom the real Truth of the matter. Security or abundance is not found in the material world.

A sense of lack is the distance we feel from our real identity, found only in the conscious awareness of the Wisdom we are and are to demonstrate. Either we honor the abundance we are, the security found only in communion with the Truth of inner Wisdom, or we honor external validation of feelings. Until we fully comprehend that only One really exists, we will try to find what we think is the real one by looking outside ourselves for our identity. But that is not where real identity can be found. How can identity be properly nestled in illusion?

With such thinking as evidence, some would say our lives are "inherited" from our parents. What we have inherited is the propensity for rendering false images real. This pattern gives entry to the Scriptural inference that the sins of our fathers are passed on to us. The "sin" spoken of here is the memory of some erroneous pattern we carry that needs to be unsettled and replaced. Lest they become idols, these false images that parent untruth must simply be acknowledged in order to set them free. What is healed by their release is the way we have seen them. Then the Truth we hear by stilling them can be worshipped in their wake. There is no room for both. Just as there is not God and something else, there is no Truth *and* error. Only One really exists. The other is imagined to be true. To believe otherwise is to relentlessly insist on, and continue parenting or bringing to Life, further ideas of duality. These configurations of ego consciousness are what seem to capture our Spirit. They serve in rendering us blind to the Truth of our Being. These, among others, work to distract us from living from our seat of spiritual consciousness.

Living largely behind a veil of ego consciousness brings on or creates forgetfulness. Fixed there, we depend on those false memories or imaginary images we took on early in our lives. They further create or parent the ways we think, feel, and react or respond to what we believe Life brings us. Only spiritual awareness can prompt needed change. Should we become aware of the need and the means, we can eventually see a clear spiritual path and walk it with our head held high.

From the reference of ego consciousness, if we feel we have been abandoned by our father or mother we will extend those feelings experienced as pain and suffering into our daily lives on many levels. It doesn't matter whether the sense of abandonment is emotional or physical, whether as a fetus or beyond. As long as we stay attached to those feelings and images, it is those that will affect how we deal with others. To the degree we feel some reconnection to the fear of abandonment happening yet again, we are bound to repeat them in our relationships. The feelings of fear seem to paralyze us, as well as the potential for healthy relationships. Unless we deal with them, we become socially crippled by them and are never able to have healthy relationships with anyone.

When we do face such emotional charges, they can alert us to erroneous levels of consciousness. If we then look at them spiritually, we come to see that the real abandonment we fear is from our real Self. When acknowledged and accepted, such awareness takes us to a deeper comprehension of how our fear images have clouded the Truth from view. We make a significant breakthrough into spiritual presence. From this newfound perch of spiritual surety, we are freed to move on to other aspects of this same treasure trove. Once blind, we can now see. Once crippled, we can now cast our various emotional crutches aside, and are free to walk unaided in Truth.

To risk redundancy here, none of this history matters. The only thing that matters relates to our one and only purpose: to become aware of and activate the spiritual Truth heard in the inner voice of Wisdom. Becoming adept at this will render all the rest unnecessary. That which parents only Truth is what animates me spiritually. What else could possibly matter?

Delivered into ego consciousness

Moving beyond prenatal influence, we find a wide array of mental configurations imposed on us from the collective weight of mass belief and opinion. From the standpoint of a belief in duality, we could speak about birth and death, for example. Some call this the definition of unconsciousness, because, mired in it, we forget the eternality and immortality of the divine consciousness we are.

In the spiritual or metaphysical tongue, however, we never refer to birth and death, for neither the spiritual nor the metaphysical is measured or defined physically. The terms spiritual and metaphysical refer only to eternal Life, meaning that divine idea or conscious awareness of Wisdom and the spiritual meaning of Life are eternal. The only thing God or

Wisdom gives birth to is an infinite stream of inspirational ideas, often referred to as divine inspiration, even grace. Thus the inspirational ideas available to us are eternal and infinite, just as they are omniscient, omnipotent, omnipresent and ever active. The only thing that dies is an old belief or opinion, suddenly replaced by a newborn inspiration. All the rest of Life is the outcome of divine ideas consciously demonstrated.

Now that we have come to gnow the real meaning of Life, we can affirm that physical death has no place in it. To believe otherwise is to affirm a belief in separation from our divine essence, and that duality is real. This would be to construct, and live from, yet another dualistic element, one to falsely worship.

To top that, we find the real meaning of death by looking closely at Life itself. Real Life is nothing but conscious awareness of divine essence, Wisdom, the only Truth for us. Being "no thing" but inspirational ideas, where might the meaning of death be found? Divine consciousness exists eternally. If not found in Life, where must we find the idea of death? Only in the illusions contained in duality, the "nether world" or dream fantasia. As we gnow by now, these fail the test of spiritual Truth.

Briefly, I will add another layer for your consideration: the death we dread is merely a metaphor for our misunderstanding that ideas fade away, seemingly to die. We are hardly versed in looking inward for the Truth of the matter, so when we feel like something is dying, even to the degree we are, indeed some *idea* of us *is* dying, about to let go. It is that clear sense of death that alerts us to the fact that change is on its way—spiritually, that is. Yet, because we are not usually aware of this phenomenon, we misinterpret it to mean we are dying physically. I speak from the authority of personal experience in this regard, so I can put you on guard as fair warning. Do not panic about feelings related to death, or even about being given a "death sentence" in health terms. Its spiritual meaning is that some idea of you, or another you have erroneously taken on from outer authority, is about to leave. Indeed, you will be transcending beyond it soon, to be resurrected into a new life, absent the old configuration of error.

Relying on fear, the ego or duality is based on the elements of difference and separation. It relies on these elements for its very existence, accompanied by feelings of guilt. No matter whether we are speaking about relationships or a sense of power and achievement, these naturally come into play. Of course, it follows that if we are feeling guilty we think we must be punished. Such strong feelings are false images, yet we feel we must deal with them. They feel too difficult or too painful to deal with inwardly, so we project them out onto the screen of our dream world. Thus, when feeling separate, we strive for relationships we think can fix that feeling for us—that can make us feel we are more complete and win for us some magical way of living.

Unfortunately, for the most part just the opposite happens: at the end of the relational rainbow we find no pot of gold, not even the bright colors that drew our attention in the first place. Instead, we find darkness illustrated by bare existence. We still feel incomplete, hollow, and unfulfilled. The magical cure we sought has not worked, characterized by infatuation with material collections, including collections of past lovers, jobs, and disappointments—all subtle forms of punishment we inflict on ourselves. And all out of a belief in a self that is separate from God, separate from what we really are.

It is from this same feeling of separation that has us competing for all we are worth, just so we can feel worthy. Much of the time we compete just to knock someone down, so we can finally feel "good enough" by falsely elevating ourselves. One day, when more aware, we find that the only place we can find our sense of completeness and being "good enough" is in spiritual Truth. Only under that government can we live in the freedom that comes to us from faithfully exercising inspirational Truth. This awareness is the beginning of a marvelous walk home, to the only location of purpose and fulfillment.

Interestingly, when feeling homeless—even when acting homelessness out in daily life—what's really happening is that we are exchanging objects of sense for quality of soul. Feeling that materialistic life is not "where it's at," we give way to living without any collections whatsoever. We make our home through attachment to "nothing at all," sensing that this is a better quality of Life than the material. When one comes to see that the new outer condition now reflects a longing for soul in place of material, this spiritual awareness frees him up to return to the only real home there is: one's inner Truth, heard in the still small voice.

The profound calling to come home is one that scares ego consciousness to death—and it begins to feel like death to us. Actually, this feeling is the beginning of the end of the powerful influence false beliefs and opinions have on us. It is not about the illusions they are, but about the power we have given to the illusions. This comes about mostly as the result of the outward influence of mass false belief in them.

Gnow this for certain: ego consciousness is not the way Jesus spoke of when he said, "I am the way, the truth, and life." Neither is it the path through the eye of the needle that sews the seamless garment of Truth for us. In reality, neither ego consciousness nor duality is a real path at all. They are only erroneous ideas believed in. Indeed, to believe Jesus meant he, as a person, is the way, the truth, and life is to pair duality with Truth. No, it is exercising conscious awareness of inner Wisdom that is the single way, the only Truth, and One Life for all. When we comprehend Jesus' admonitions spiritually, we come to gnow that this is the Truth of which he spoke.

In its fear state the illusory voice of duality will tempt us, bargain with us, flatter us and bribe us, wanting survival in return. One way you can be sure duality exists as a counter influence is that its ways appear more and more regularly in everyday existence. It is quite simple to discern, really. If you find these false images "in your face," you can be sure it is ego trying to retain your loyalty in the only ways it has available. The good news is that your increased awareness of this false imagery is a sure sign you are readily moving into the One and only, divine awareness. Use these signs, then, to point you precisely—and only—in that direction, to that place of divine Being.

The Scriptural reference here is when Jesus was tempted by the ego—called evil or the devil, the temptress by some—for those forty days and nights in the desert. Jesus dealt with his demons, first, by recognizing them and denying them access. He turned them away, saying "Get thee behind me, Satan." Then, after he had recognized the subtle and not so subtle advances for what they were, he simply walked away from them, onto the path where only inner Truth prevails. From then on, it was on this path of Oneness that he traveled.

How much more evidence do we need in order to understand Jesus' admonition: "It is not I but the Father within that speaks, that does these things?" Again, in the tongue we now speak, the silent language of divine consciousness expressed, Jesus' declaration sounds like this: "It is not I, but my awareness of the divine Wisdom within that speaks, that activates Life for me." Add to that, "I can of my own self do nothing," and we see that Jesus' teachings are perfect. They attribute all activation of Truth to the conscious awareness of, and commitment to, the demonstration of Wisdom, The Inward Way. It is a Life of active awareness that parents or fathers real Life into activation. Indeed, inspiration breathes Spiritual meaning into Life.

If we are to follow Jesus' stunning revelations, the path we are to tread is one of obedience or surrender to those very same Truths. Life can never be the same when we experience this. Even if Jesus only symbolically represents a certain level of consciousness of which we are to become aware, the intent of allegorical meaning is clear. We thus can abort any need to find out whether the Bible is literally true or simply a collection of allegories that lead us to Truth.

We "cannot see the face of God and live," we are told. The spiritual reality of this expression is that once we see the face of God—that is, consciously experience the Truth of Wisdom as the spiritual path—we can no longer live in the false belief in ego or mass consciousness. We will have found our home in—and as— the Truth we find there. The Truth represented is so profoundly evident that obedience or surrender to it is the only natural response. No longer does the ego form of duality exist; neither does the false idea of choice that comes with it.

Let this mediation of the story of Jesus put you on notice that Truth spoken *is* the journey here. In Jesus' own words, he came not to change Scripture but to mediate it. He treated it in the way it was intended: as spiritual—as the One and only idea of spiritual consciousness and divine order. The infinitude of spiritual ideas contained in Wisdom renders the letter or literal meaning of the law as the illusion found in outer authority. As you see other references to Jesus' words here, if you will hold them in this same context your view of Life will never again be the same. Grace will have set you free from past misunderstandings that no longer serve you.

We have nothing to fear but fear itself

President Franklin Delano Roosevelt had it right when he uttered these words long ago in a time of war. The force that keeps us captive and clouds us from the "high road" upon which we are meant to tread is the huge influence of fear. Fear of both failure and success; fear of becoming aware of our True selves; fear of all those yesterdays repeating themselves today or in some imagined future; fear of the ideas of both Life and death; fear that we will be abandoned; fear of lack; and on the list goes, seemingly forever. These are typical of the ways a belief in ego and mass consciousness holds us prisoner to fear.

Fear is what keeps us in debilitating jobs or relationships;

what seems to make us give up our souls to others; what cripples us from moving forward; holds us in some form of current dysfunction or sends us backward into our equally-dysfunctional past. Fear is a killer, which brings increased levels of tension into our lives. In the life of ego consciousness, it is that very tension which shifts our bodily chemistry for the worse. And from bad chemistry comes disease in the human realm. This bad chemistry that emanates from fear, worry, angst, and other fearful emotions is opposed to the peace of mind found only in our spiritual core.

It is important to remember that each time we rehearse a debilitating story or unfounded fear we are also reinforcing the "chemistry" that comes from it. Thus, the toxicity trapped in our physical structure grows and is reinforced. The key, then, is to release it by giving it no thought whatsoever, no matter how it shows up. Simply acknowledge it, bid it a farewell, and then go on living what you know to be true, living *nothing but that Truth.*

Quoting from an earlier work that came through me (re-paragraphed now by the author),*"THE CREATION SPIRIT; Expressing Your Divinity in Everyday Life,"* this is what comes of belief in fear:

"We can also come to our understanding of the purity of Loving by the perception of that which does its best to keep us from Loving: fear. Fear seems to have power over us. It can render us so-called insane. Fear is the greatest of demons.

In all kinds of insidious ways fear keep us from moving forward. Fear seduces us into staying in places and relationships that are no longer appropriate for us. Fear keeps us from telling the truth to both ourselves and to others. It blocks us from standing up to bullies and others who abuse us. It keeps us in jobs that have long since passed their usefulness. It keeps us from even the simplest decisions, for fear of being wrong—or right. Fear keeps us from acting in the simplicity of kindness, fearing we will be stepped on, abandoned, or rejected yet one more time.

Prolonged, suppressed fear turns into anger, then depression, sending us to our real or imagined bed in escape from the decisions and changes we must face within ourselves. Eventually it can even coax us to end life in this body. Fear blinds us, cripples us, it makes us think we're going crazy. Fear deadens our Spirit. Fear is a killer.

Relationally it keeps us from dealing justly with ourselves and with others...Fear, the cleverest and most powerful weapon of mortal mind (ego), keeps us from our Truth, from living authentically and genuinely as the True Self we Are, from being authentically Loving...It is in Oneness, and not fear, that we come to at last fulfill the sacredness of human dignity." (p. 82-83)

Such a summary renders fear as the ego-like villain it is. A belief in ego consciousness is filled with such villains, mostly thinly disguised impostors like doubt and angst, yet all are fear-related to be sure. What is the way out of this fix we seem to be in? As Joel Goldsmith puts it, "nothingize it." Make nothing out of each ego conscious thought that comes into view, for each is founded in some erroneous belief or opinion. Thus ego conscious thought is nothing (no thing) at all, only a figment of our waking dream world.

In the Gospel of John (14:27), Jesus said this to us about fear: "Let your heart not be troubled, neither let it be afraid." Could there be a more powerful entreaty than this to point out that the very fear we feel permeating ego consciousness is to be avoided at all cost and, if not, that our hearts will be troubled? Yes, it is this same troubled heart that is our cue, and clue, to remember, yet again, to return to the awareness of our one and only Truth. "To thine own Self be True," Shakespeare told us. It is an admonition we might use to our spiritual advantage, and to help form our legacy.

Eventually, we come to the realization that our real task as the tentative holders of a belief in the ego consciousness model is to overcome the unreality of fear. And then we do what we must out of the Truth of our Being. By overcoming our belief in fear, we will have put behind us the illusory idol of Satan. Once the veil has been cleared, real Life unfolds before us. Suddenly we see the Truth of our Being, which necessitates that we live from nothing other than that. We finally become aware that there is nothing else *to* be expressed.

By now you may well have come to the identical conclusion that I have about fear: when we experience Life unconsciously or out of a belief in ego consciousness, fear is the "director" of the never-ending play we call drama. Drama comes in all sizes, shapes, and colors. Of this we can be sure: as a perfect reflection of our belief in ego consciousness, drama is never-ending. As a matter of fact, when you see someone in the midst of drama, or "calling drama to themselves" on a regular basis, this is most assuredly a sign that belief in ego consciousness is at work. Some might not agree with this characterization, perhaps because they are blinded by the inherent qualities of ego consciousness: separation and fear. Do you mean to tell me that an empty existence filled only with a compelling sense of separation and fear is not drama waiting for the curtain to rise?

It is likely that most of us do not think we are living one drama after another, simply because many of the dramas surface quickly and effortlessly and are gone as soon as we see the unnatural disturbance in them. As soon as this untoward appearance begins to surface, those who are more aware turn to the high road, walking around the impending drama to inner peace on the other side. This takes courage to see the difference between drama and inner peace, and it takes obedience or surrender to walk around potential drama to the Truth of the matter, despite the tugs from past habits.

Drama is a debilitating influence. It tends to pull down anyone who attaches himself to any of the attendant roles. Drama's purpose, just as it is for the belief in ego consciousness which parents it, is to pull any who participate down to its own lowly level. It is the only way someone who is embroiled in drama can get any sense of worth, a glimpse of importance, some attention, or feeling of equality. So, be aware of what is happening around you and, even more important, to what's happening within you.

When you have some sense that the drama pot is heating up, it is a sure sign to back up and gain another, more wholesome, perspective, which will turn the stove of ego consciousness off so you can cool down. I hope it is now clear to you that dramas are something to gain your attention, whether it is one brewing in you or someone else. The good news in this is that dramas are a clear indication of ego consciousness at work, and they can point us, when we are aware, to the need for remembering the Truth of our Being.

Again, if we stay aware we can easily see when and how this insidious belief in ego consciousness is operating. Each time we can say with abundant clarity and the power of Truth: "Get thee behind me, Satan. Divine consciousness is the only God I worship. There is no other." As we continue this journey together, we'll see how the following principles work to this spiritual end.

The implications of technology

Just as our personal relationships show us our current state of consciousness and point to ways of returning to our only path of inner Truth, so does the vast spectrum of so-called technological advancement. As with other entries in this chapter, a narrow view of technological advancement provides a handy distraction from facing our fears.

We take on the inventions of "blue-tooth" technology, for example, only to learn that its use can be cancer producing. Yet we ignore such warnings; our thought of convenience is the one we worship. Much like the old cathode ray tubes in earlier TV appliances, we ignore the radiation in favor of convenience and entertainment value. Actually, television becomes a symbol for the inner ability to "raise up" images from anywhere in the Universe, simply by connecting with, or tuning into, our infinite imagination.

In the case of "blue-tooth" technology, not unlike with computers, such technological "advances" speak to the highly complex nature of our own inner awareness. There is nothing we really *need* that is not readily available from within, simply by listening for the Truth rendered in the still, small voice. I like to call this spiritual telepathy. If we practiced communicating through devotion to inner listening as much as we expend energy sorting out the plethora of information available on the Internet, I am convinced that we would need fewer words to effectively communicate. Instead, we would come to know what is being communicated in the language God speaks: Wisdom found in silence. How many of us already have witnessed a seemingly sudden inner connection to someone, only to have the phone ring and find her on the other end of the line? How many of us find ourselves completing sentences begun by a friend or loved one before they finish them? Or know what they are going to say even before they open their mouth? Of course, we all have witnessed such signs. The point is, if we would only quiet our daily existence and allow ourselves the spaciousness to hear what already is, we would be free from the perceived need to say much aloud at all. Think of how much time that would free up to just Be!

Not only are we already able to access all Wisdom necessary for fruitful living, it is instantly available. Yet again, so we can see how we are ignoring interior Life, our desire to obtain more powerful computers with even more sophisticated systems for communicating faster is but an out-picturing or metaphor calling our attention to Truth. *Whatever* calls us in the way of metaphor or symbolism serves an essential spiritual purpose in addition to the one made evident in physical form. It shows us some spiritual Truth physically, so those of us who are unaware of the fullness of spiritual power and inner gnowing can be alerted to it through physical example. Truly, as we learn to see outer appearances also as spiritual metaphors, we can access the depth of spiritual meaning and Life regularly, rather than only sporadically.

So-called technological advances continue to raise important questions for me. For example, have we not previously lived fruitful lives without a cell-phone attached to our ear or a computer hooked to Internet on our lap? The answer to that question is as clear as the noonday sun on a cloudless summer day. It is no big deal, really: as long as we keep our focus on discerning outward manifestation as the "confessional" for inner Truth, and keep our existence in the world of technology in balance, we will be well served on our spiritual journey.

By over-emphasizing the qualities of digital photography, e.g., immediate gratification, easy storage, and quick time sharing, we could well be distracted from the symbolic meaning of the process of photography itself. Metaphysically speaking, photography is about seeing Life from different perspectives, and reframing it so we can come to new awareness. It is much like coming to understand an earlier career in higher education: it wasn't about more education and accumulating paper degrees but about gaining deeper meaning. It is for this that we view the world outside us, as the mirror of appearance that reflects inner meaning.

From a strictly practical point of view, the bottom line on the technological explosion is that although we can be assisted by such things, what they are for the most part is a distraction from living in the now as well as from going within for the Truth of our Being. Spiritually speaking, any device that takes us to external authority in favor of inner validation and affirmation is a diversion from our real path. The more time we spend on Internet and/or on email—often substituting glib and superficial messages for substantial communication—the less we focus our attention on the here and now, and with developing the personal and spiritual relationships on which spiritual Life thrives. I dare say that no one really thrives spiritually who is consumed by the trivialities and banalities of the technological plane. The thought of staying stuck in this frame of reference makes me shudder to think what the face of authentic communication could look like a generation from now.

Despite the fact that these technological advances might well be characterized as plain and simple "convenience," the question that needs to be asked is this: At what price do convenience and entertainment come? People who adhere unconsciously or out of peer pressure to such advances with all they're worth are, in a sense, worshipping false idols.

If you are not yet convinced, just take a few moments to trace your own steps in this regard. How much money have you spent on such devices? How much more time and energy do you spend on your cell phone than you did with a regular landline? And is it of greater or less quality for time invested? How much time do you spend on Internet looking for information that really only "sucks you in" to the appeal it has in this format? How much money, time, and energy do you spend using technological gadgets when the good old-fashioned way uses our minds and bodies in much healthier and more wholesome ways? I am sure you can add to the seemingly endless list of such matters and concerns. The real question to ask is: Which of these so-called choices is priceless?

A case can be made that attraction to such devices and "easy access" is nothing but temptation based on fear. Some of us fear to look within to such a huge degree that we will attach ourselves to any device or activity just to keep us from looking to the Truth of any matter. Truth is very scary to many, and when coupled by the mass consciousness influence that insists on external authority as the answer to all that troubles us, we are driven back to erroneous beliefs and opinions. None of these has anything whatsoever to do with the Truth of spiritual Life. Indeed, the corporate and industrial complexes that know this about the nature of ego consciousness feast on the benefits derived from such depravation.

This testimony is not to discredit technological advances as helpful. Rather, it is a plea to have real authority—inner authority—govern our focus, and service the spiritual way as the only real way of fulfilling our calling. The inner authority found in Wisdom will head us toward technological advances only in a balanced and healthy way. Just staying in conscious awareness of its messages in this regard is our personal and spiritual guarantee. I encourage more active infusion of inner Life as the sure cure for outer stimulation and infatuation.

The final conclusion here is identical to the one at the end of the last section. To place our belief in technology as a panacea of some kind is to argue against the Allness of God. The importance of technology is as a physical symbol that points us to the spiritual Truth we can find only in our hearts. Once in our Truth, the spiritual answers we need for fulfillment are instantaneously supplied.

Religious dogmestication

Another significant impact on our Life-view is formed by the nature of our religious upbringing. Religious indoctrination (I like to call it "dogmestication," because so often we are domesticated by religious dogma) says that we must read Scripture literally and administer it rationally. Thus, depending on the nature of religious upbringing, one could easily come to the view that God and we are separate, and that we are to beg or beckon some God "out there" to serve our every need, to whom we are to supplicate our faith in order to gain our every wish or desire.

If we were to investigate the Bible as we see it today from a spiritual basis, we would find that it formulates a god that serves the ego and substantiates duality. In the formulation that began this "translation" some 300-400 years after Jesus died, an external god serves to terrify and subjugate people. Subjugate to whom or what? To "the church" and its hierarchy. This is the paternalistic or ego-conscious and fear-based way. We see its influence not only in "the church," but also in government and in corporate or organizational life. Because ego consciousness has received so much reinforcement through our institutions, it has found its way into relationships of all kinds. Formalized religion is based on the beliefs and desires of others and has no place in spirituality. Spirituality, on the other hand, is based in experience—in our ability to experience God or Wisdom for ourselves. As we are finding out, we reach a higher level of spiritual consciousness not from largely self-serving outer belief but authentic inner Authority.

Through dogmestication, as a Christian it would be easy to believe that only God and Jesus are One, and as separate from them we are less than either or both. From this erroneous teaching we gain the perspective that we are "less than good enough," and dedicate our lives to overworking just so we might one day measure up to those around us and God alike. Either that, or we give up entirely and become the underachiever of underachievers.

I consider Jesus to have been a Master metaphysician. Primarily, only Jesus' teachings—when comprehended symboli- cally—point to the way of living spiritually. He saw God as all, and thus that we are not separate at all, neither from God nor one another. Jesus taught by example that he and his Father, the consciousness that parented all he was and did, and were One and the same. His teaching is the profound principle of at-one-ment. We are not separate from God as reinforced in much of the Bible; God and we are One. Many of Jesus' other teachings also verify this view of Oneness, yet time and again the reinforcement we obtain through indoctrination tells us the contrary. Who and what are we to believe? In the simplest terms, we are to celebrate the eternal presence, never the belief in absence, of God, of our spiritual Truth found in Wisdom.

Religiously, we are told to write Scripture on our hearts, meaning that we are to take its meaning literally to heart. Symbolically, we find the essence of Scriptural meaning only *in* our hearts. It is only there where we hear the meaning of spiritual Truth. That is the clarity or resonance we feel, which says, "yes" to us in agreement with the Truth. Yet religious leaders of all kinds and descriptions would have us lean on their translations of Scripture, and on them, for what they claim is hidden there. Religious dogma thus becomes a perpetual crutch, which also keeps us in darkness or ignorance of inner awareness—the single ultimate cure for our spiritual ills.

Of course, this builds an unhealthy dependency on religious leaders for the very foundation that nourishes soul. Should we not instead rely on the highest Self we find inward? It seems to me that for us to do otherwise would be to worship false gods. This is the Life-long argument for outside authority affixed in much of organized religion. Wisdom, found within, is the only real Authority. It is only there, in the voice of highest good, where Truth and spiritual validation are found. To separate one from the other is to live in a dualistic world. The teachings of the Master Jesus were about Oneness, not dualism.

Here is another example of an untruth perpetrated upon us: "The church" says that only God and Jesus heal, yet Jesus said that we are a society of healers. "These things shall you do; even greater than these you shall do," he said to us. Why would he have said such a thing if he or God were the only ones to heal—

the only spiritual Masters? Further to the point, when we are told of the healings Jesus performed in Scripture, they are made to sound as though all of them were instantaneous. In one sense they were, because in any healing there is a moment when the ailment or dis-ease is finished, is no more. However, through the Biblical inference of these stories, we obtain what largely is false testimony, and a superficial description of Jesus' metaphysical "healings." We are given little hint of what really transpired, hence they don't seem to resonate as Truth—so their meaning must come from a different source of comprehension.

It will suffice for now to say that Jesus healed not physical ailments so much, but rather the frailties of human under-standing—the false perspectives and beliefs we hold to be the Truth, but which are not that at all. Each of these false perspec-tives is like a crutch that holds our "dis-ease" with Life, as many of us are living it, in place. Fulfillment is found not in crutches but in expressing conscious awareness of inner Truth or Wisdom. To press the point just a little further, is it not possible that Jesus simply helped people see Life from a perspective that crippled them to another that set them free—from belief in ego consciousness to the inner authority of spiritual consciousness? Is it not spiritually possible that Jesus shifted meaning of a particular belief that held someone blind to spiritual reality into one that brought enlightenment through insight? Can we also see the possibility that Jesus helped another through a story, a symbolic representation of Truth that enabled that person to truly hear for himself—that is, to discern real meaning about his Life? Hearing spiritual meaning cleared the cripple of his deafness to the resonance of Truth heard in silence.

In essence, Jesus said to the crippled man at the pool in Bethesda that had made his bed of limitation and now he had to sleep in it. The alternative Jesus gave him was to cast that bed of old beliefs aside and walk on in his new comprehension of Life's meaning. Jesus would not have said pick up your bed and walk to the physically crippled man, for this would change nothing. Spirit does not change human condition. Rather, Jesus would be saying this to the Christ, the perfect being he saw as all. He was correcting in *his* view the appearance of the crippled man. This is the only correction that can take place. Thus it is Jesus' teaching that when we see each as the One, the perfect reflection of inner Wisdom, we will have taken the correct posture toward all, reinforcing the Truth of their being. In this way, all are without error, even if only in their spiritual form, regardless how they might see themselves.

Admittedly, it would have taken more room in the Scriptures to describe such discussions, such rich teaching. Let us think of Scripture as allegorical in nature. If we would just look at Scripture spiritually—meaning as divine ideas to be taken symbolically—then we, too, can be healed of such misperceptions. These misperceptions are what keep us crippled—what severely limit us from walking in our spiritual foundation.

I will speak to one last so-called religious reference that applies here. Just to be clear about my use of the term "the Christ," I will state emphatically that those who use the term "Jesus" and "Christ" as one and the same are incorrect in their understanding of spiritual intent. This synonymous treatment of the two comes from the literalists who use it for whatever purpose they have. Spiritually, however, "Jesus" refers to the Master teacher who serves as the living example how one regularly expresses the conscious awareness of his One and only Truth. Jesus gave to us the comprehensive understanding of what he meant by being at One with the divine consciousness that parented him. "The Christ," on the other hand, is the inherent, immortal and infinite consciousness each of us is, and what we are to demonstrate or manifest moment by moment. It is that still, small voice we hear, where the real "I" resides. We are not a physical body, but the embodiment of inspiration or divine consciousness individualized, the One and only "I." At last, we are neither lost nor sought, for in our Truth we are found—as the Christ we are, our highest Self heard within.

As we open ourselves to the real meaning of Jesus' teachings, contrary to how others might see them—or want us to see them—Jesus did not see others simply as having the divine in them. No, he saw all *as* divine. In that sacred frame of reference, Jesus saw all as divine consciousness, and thus in need of healing not at all. How could something so perfect, all powerful, eternal, and immortal need healing? Can you envision God with a cold or the flu, or as a leper? "Be ye perfect, even as God in Heaven is perfect." "I and my father are one." Each sacred idea is formed out of divine consciousness. This means now, in the present moment, not at some later time or place. Inspiration is the resonance felt, the Truth heard and the real meaning comprehended. It comes in an instant, the present. This is the real manna from Heaven, the purest meaning found only in Wisdom. It is the food of which earthlings gnow not.

The examples above show how, in our past, we might have been distracted from spiritual reality in favor of some external authority. Investing our Truth in the hands of external authority may have shielded our eyes from that which lies within as the only Truth for us. It is primarily this very shield that installs and perpetuates us in a Life unfulfilled and lacking a sense of purpose. It is because of this shield that we feel disconnected and empty, essentially hollow inside. Indeed, the shield blinds us to the one and only real relationship with the God expressed as all, the One. You are that, and so am I that, God or Wisdom individually expressed. "I am that; I am," remember.

Transitioning to ultimate Truth

Without risking our lives to duality, we can transition to a more complete understanding of our spiritual or divine consciousness by taking more seriously the admonition that we are created in the image and likeness of God. So many of us take that to mean that God is like us, looks like us, and is either masculine or feminine—or both. Yet, out of the leanings of the religious patriarchy we use the term "He" for God. Of late, in our drive for gender equality (as though God were a human, with gender), we call God, Father-Mother God.

In fact, the image and likeness of God means that we are the same quality—the same divine essence as God or Wisdom—no different in any way. We have and reflect the same attributes; how could we not if we truly are One? The divine idea of us is what is real. Only those who forget what they really are behave as something they truly are not. Such behavior is a clear sign of belief in the absence of God's omnipresence, omnipotence, omniscience, and ever-activeness—a belief in a self apart from God, apart from the voice of Wisdom.

A simple way of coming to grips with these challenging words and ideas is to take out a good dictionary and find the description of God. Begin with a literal understanding and then reach beyond that to the deeper meaning. Write down those words used to display God's attributes and then find synonyms for them, followed by what defines them for you. Then, make a simple chart with those attributes on one side, with enough room for you to comment alongside each descriptor. Finally, by using spiritual discernment—that is, by listening within—write down how you display those very characteristics and attributes.

The final outcome? At the very least, you will find the similarity between how God and you manifest these same behaviors. These are what identifies character and from which Wisdom is clarified. Actually, this exercise is to help you more fully comprehend that when you give Life to your individualization of Wisdom you come to fully understand that, "I and my Father are One." Once having seen this, the words used to define us the same do not really matter. Are we getting any closer to the Truth about the *real* you?

In this regard, I note this very comparison, found in *THE*

CREATION SPIRIT:
"We exhibit life when we let our creative juices flow, creating lovingly at every opportunity. We exhibit ardor when we unleash burning desire and unbridled enthusiasm for our given purpose in Life. We exhibit courage every time we look fear in the eye and move through fear to loving creativity on the other side. We are immaterial, intelligent substance every time we get out of our own controlling ways and let God work through us. We are the soul of humankind, in likeness with all others, when we open ourselves fully to another in celebration of the gift Life is." (p. 65)

By living our calling faithfully we provide all with our spiritual authenticity. We are called to openly, confidently, and authentically individualize our spiritual reality. When doing so, others also are emboldened and ennobled in their very own spiritual way. After all, this gift of grace is given for a more Universal purpose.

Before leaving this section, I'll ask just one question: So? So what? Precisely: sow what we really are and none else. All of the religious and spiritual teachings, including most of those listed here, have no real meaning for us at all. The only real meaning comes—you guessed it—when we listen in our heart of hearts. Follow only that meaning; silence your beliefs and opinions; and "all the rest will be given unto you." Wisdom can give only what it is, after all. And then we can give the Universe the very same.

Serial relationships

Because we are led to believe that we are separate from one another and God, we have let that mass consciousness lead us to deep feelings of separation, and all the pain and sorrow that separation engenders. It places us on a win-lose fulcrum, leaving us feeling that we're up one minute and down the next. It is incumbent upon us to shatter the old images that continue to haunt us. Only then will there be room for the new to enter.

Understand one thing: when feeling separate—founded on an erroneous belief system—we tend to look everywhere but within to be completed. We fall in love we say, but we really are simply infatuated with the idea of someone else completing us; making us whole. We suffer through one work relationship or through one career or another, only to eventually find out that it is really not those that make us whole or give us our identity. The dualistic world is based on competition of some kind, witnessed by nothing but one win-lose scenario after another. From this bed of duality we like to think that our thoughts create our reality, and we exercise that false belief regularly, in all kinds of forms. And we stay stuck in duality, as long as we refuse to listen within our hearts for the only Truth about Life. Spiritually, the only sound relationship is the one we lovingly bond with in the depths of our hearts. When we fall in love with the voice heard in stillness and obey or surrender to Wisdom faithfully, all the rest—an infinite supply of more and more Wisdom—is given unto us. All that could possibly be given in the name of real love finds its way to our feet. We need not give any other relationship thought. Genuine relationship begins at home, in the enlightened state that speaks as us. When followed, all relationships are created in the image and likeness of this primary sacred One, and Life changes dramatically for the better. Actually, Life does not change at all. It is we who change the way we see Life, and thus what meaning we give to Life. And all around us are affected in similar fashion.

My all-time favorite story in this regard is about a dear friend who sent me a revelatory email indicating that she had just severed her relationship with yet another fellow. Following prayerful reflection, she said this: " I just knew it was right to let go. I said the words. It felt real. Then I was thinking about being sought instead of seeking someone. And I thought, 'I don't want to be sought any more. I want to be found.' And then I had a profound experience of feeling I AM. I was once lost but NOW, I AM found. And here I AM, in this moment. My heart feels so full again. Grace is an amazing thing!" And so is this story. To be aware of Oneness, and to live from that spaciousness, is reality found. Indeed, grace is amazing!

Margaret Marshall, a friend who engages metaphysics at every opportunity, recently shared this with me, a statement that came out of her awareness of the only real relationship:

"Do not judge your family, your friends, or the strangers that you meet in your daily life. They, like you, are on a journey that offers its challenges and its blessings. These challenges are unique to each of us. What you see in others is evident only for the moment in which you view them. Each new day can bring changes that will be imperceptible to you and possibly to them. Then consider that what you might be seeing in them and in yourself are fleeting shadows of a perfection that is hidden from view.

Maybe it is time to begin seeing yourself, and everyone, not in a transitional state but in a complete state that has a built in oneness with the Father and that was established 'in the beginning' and remains unchanged throughout eternity."

What a simple, yet profound, way of seeing Life spiritually this is—and such a profound way of establishing and maintaining our commitment to divine relationship. As paraphrased from Proverbs (27:19), "As water reflects a face, so a man's heart reflects the man." It is from the heart, the Truth found there, that we find the only real relationship to be divine. And it is through this unchanging face of Truth that we demonstrate our conscious awareness of Wisdom to all.

I gnow this much: I gnow that if I do not go within, I go without—without the Truth for me, that is. Without is never where the Truth is found. If I fail to go within to the seat of Wisdom that resides in me, I am depriving myself of divine consciousness, what has only highest good at heart. This is the "Soul" that beckons me to live faithfully to my integrity of Being. In this is dignity rendered sacred and whole. And it is in this form only that we express the integrity of divine relationship. "To thine own self be true." Letting go of everything that limits this approach is all that is necessary to activate spiritual authenticity.

With eyes to see

As we begin to replace those shopworn images, which have virtually guaranteed our current place in a largely dysfunctional society, with our Truth, we come to reflect what conscious awareness of Wisdom inspires in us. The more we become aware of our Truth and practice it, the more our heart opens to the Kingdom that is our inheritance. Actually, the Kingdom of divine inspiration found in Wisdom is our inherent nature. All its good awaits our awareness and activation.

There are many more ways we have come to see Life as debilitating, or at least largely unsatisfactory. You can use the prior examples to unloose others, so you can begin to let them go and live spiritually instead. Because the listing of those factors which might have impacted your Life are largely negative, it occurs to me that you may come to the conclusion that there are only a few good influences, at best, that surround us. Rest assured, this is not so. There is much that reminds us of our Truth, much that lets us see how we are fulfilling Life in a spiritually exemplary way.

In this helter-skelter world we live in today, where so many of us are in some kind of race with time, the good all too easily escapes our attention, blurred by the fast-paced lifestyle we have chosen. The principles which follow will awaken you to your Truth in ways that could well establish a new habit of acknowledging and demonstrating the "spiritual you" on a more regular basis. When we learn that we are really a speed bump instead of a roadrunner, we'll slow down enough so we remember to express what we really are.

I take this moment to emphasize this Truth that guides me on my way: all these factors that appear to hinder us on our way are entirely inconsequential. It is only our belief in them—and in the need to remove every one of them before we are whole—that keeps us in them, in the illusion of our past. It is this fixation that gives them power. Rest assured that being in the present moment with our Truth is all that is necessary to escape the bonds of this waking dream, this illusion. For example, once we see that the memories of the past are illusions and thus not real, all the fears that accompany them disappear instantaneously. Belief in any outer source—and our never-ending thoughts about it, like belief in suffering—creates and maintains precisely what we seek to avoid. Belief in the potentiality of some past repeating itself does exactly the same thing: it holds us in the fear once felt. Not only are we held there; as long as we hold onto the painful thought, we will stay in the suffering to which it speaks. The process of living our perfection of Being is thus reduced to living what we are moment by moment. Indeed, once we come to gnow that divine consciousness is the only thing on the spiritual menu, we fret no longer about the need to choose from a long list of illusory items in a wilting buffet of illusion. Nor do we fear the consequences of choice, because the Truth sets us free from the illusion of choice. Given spiritual context, only adherence to inner purpose is available to us as highest good.Be wary of suggestions that living only from the single vision of Truth would be boring or would not really work. Such a declaration or belief is just another argument against the allness and richness of Wisdom lived. Besides, who among us has consistently practiced it? How can abiding what we really are be anything but enlightening, and thus uplifting? It is by abiding transcendence that we are free to express spiritual Life enthusiastically.

I just love it when someone bent on intellect and rationality as the provider of Truth argues for collecting vast arrays of information—all of it, true or false—as the means for arriving at some desired solution. Collect it all, they say, and it will inform intuition. Long ago and far away, before the advent of newspapers and other purveyors of information, including libraries, both material and electronic, how did wise people arrive at the Truth for them? Is intuition only a recent discovery? The term "intuition" might be a recent discovery, but I remain convinced that wise ones always simply got out of their own way and let Truth speak. And they did it for simple and complex concerns alike, not as some afterthought.

Somehow we have been led to the conclusion that insight and rationality are equals in their ability to guide us in living spiritually. I ask only this: just how well has this conclusion worked for you lately? Why not open up to a different way, even if only to see for yourself if it can work? Each of us knows the value of intuition and insight, yet we generally abandon it for a more rational approach. It is like first trying everything we know to do, only to find out that none of it has worked—and then praying to God as a last resort. Why not visit inwardly *first*, for what Wisdom has to say?

Begin now simply by drinking in these examples and principles, continually exercising your inherent ability to go within to find Truth's resonance there. The single requirement is to listen within for your direction—the resonance you hear there—and you will find that Life will look very different to you. Even more importantly, it will *be* very different for you.

I will conclude this chapter with a story. This one comes from Yakov, an American comedian of Russian decent performing in Branson, Missouri. He tells of a conversation with a couple celebrating their sixtieth wedding anniversary. Asking the woman what she attributes the longevity of their relationship to, she responds, "He makes me laugh, and I just love that in him." Yakov then asks the husband the same question, and he responds, "Oh, she laughs at my stories, and I just adore that in her." The point of his story, so far, is that it's genuine give and take that makes for sound relationships. And we need not take ourselves too seriously as we traverse the planet together.

As the story continues, Yakov asks the woman what else there might be that helped hold their loving relationship in place. Not hesitating at all, she responds, "Well, you know most men don't like to get directions when traveling somewhere. Despite that, he knows I'd like him to check from time to time, just to comfort me. So, on occasion, he pulls into a gasoline station to inquire. I just love that in him." (Incidentally, it is ego, and not masculinity, that rests in self-righteousness. It is misunderstanding that lands the false claim in the lap of men. But that is a discussion for another day.)

Yakov goes on to say that there is a basis for her statement about men not wanting to get directions, even if grounded in story. "We all know that usually only one of thousands of sperm reaches the fertile egg," he says, "but do you know why that's the case? Only one stopped for directions." Spiritually, the virtue of the story is this: how can we possibly consummate our communion with Wisdom if we do not faithfully follow the proper direction to get there?

As with all that seems to trouble us in the world of appearance, pay it no mind. Give it no thought. Only commune in secret at the seat of Wisdom you are sure to find in your inner closet, shutting the door to all else behind you. The "all else behind you," consists of all those shopworn beliefs and opinions that no longer apply. Only Truth does now.

Chapter Three

Principle 1: When you become aware of *what* you really are, you'll be what you really want to see

"My silences become more accurate."
Theodore Roethke

Belief into reality

The first thing I would like you to gnow about this principle is that it is the Truth. Those who gnow me well also gnow I like to take others to the seat of their own Truth, so I will extend this view into a spiritual perspective. I will say this in spiritual terms: what you Be is what you really are. Forgive this illiterate substitute for correct grammar. But you get the point, I am sure. If you want to find out the Truth of your Being you must first become aware of *who* you are not, so you can see *what* you really are. You can then behave or manifest Life from that deeper level of comprehension.

Having said that, if you want to find out *who* you are, you are looking in the right place. This worldly consciousness consists of dualistic, ego-materialistic illusion, a consciousness fulfilled through the illusory roles we play. Unfortunately, we mostly take on our roles as our real identity. And we take ourselves way too seriously! The only thing is, there are not two powers, divine consciousness and ego consciousness. The latter is only a figment of our belief in it, and thus not real at all.

Collective or mass consciousness perpetrates and perpetuates duality when we are unaware. When you find yourself saying, "I just do not know who I am anymore," or asking, "Is this all there is to life?" this is a sure sign that it is your inner Self, soul, calling you to the full awareness of what you really are. We need that "bump in the night" to awaken us to the only real Life. This spiritual calling will inform you that all you thought you wanted is not anything real and therefore cannot last. All the houses and all the money and all the cars and, yes, even all the love relationships in the world can neither satisfy nor ever make you happy.

Only by living in the Truth of our spiritual consciousness can we truly be happy. Here is why: because conscious awareness of what we really are, *is* happiness and joy; it *is* abundance; it *is* peace of mind. All these are natural characteristics and attributes we find when we abandon illusion. The real Truth can be no less. Simply put, the material world is not the place to seek spiritual completion. All we strive for outside us only speaks to seeing happiness through roles we play rather than understanding that we are, and always have been, happiness as a divine idea. Our belief in, or consciousness of, the material realm cannot provide these, for they are not in the same world most of us live in. Jesus said this: "My kingdom (my Life, my consciousness) is not of this world." In the tongue of metaphysics, it could well be read as "My Life is of Spirit, Wisdom expressed as inspiration, not of the senses, not of the material, not of these false idols, like ego and collective consciousness." The distinction Jesus made was abundantly clear, especially because he was speaking spiritually and not materially.

So when you change how you see to the spiritual way, what you see will be the Truth about real Life. How can this be? Because your sight will have changed from material to spiritual, and spiritual is the only perfect vision. Your way of seeing will have changed from literally or intellectually seeing something to gaining insight and enlightenment. If you want this perfect vision, spiritual 20/20 vision, you must go within, for only you can provide yourself with perfect spiritual vision by going into silence, where insight and enlightenment emanate from Wisdom—where the divine consciousness you are resides, waiting only for an opportunity to be heard as the perfection it is—and you are.

Life begins with listening for intuition—the clear, full awareness of only highest good. Life arrives as we set ourselves free from a belief in the dualistic imagery of ego consciousness, essentially letting Truth have its way with us. As we fully comprehend this inner meaning, we are brought into the perfection of Being we always have been, erasing once and for all the ego consciousness trait of forgetfulness.

You can help yourself in many ways. One way often suggested is to follow this admonition: "God helps those who help themselves." Unfortunately, this is only a half-baked ego-centered idea. The more wholesome variety is: "God helps those who help themselves—by going within for help." There is a big difference between these two forms of admonition. The first leads us to rugged individuality and the idea that we can think or work ourselves into the right thing for us. This is the way that comes from a belief in ego consciousness and is rendered as self-righteousness. In the dualistic world, we have no real idea what is best for us—none. How do we shift from this false belief? Paraphrasing Jesus, he said to us, "Give it no thought." The longer statement is "Not one of you can add one cubit of good to your life through thought." His meaning is clear enough, is it not?

Truth be gnown

What is the key to becoming more aware? Just as a reminder of what you already know about yourSelf, if you only go within for the Truth of the matter, you will quickly come to gnow (a) *who* you are not! And that will tell you *what* you are. Lord gnows, we have labored under the untruth of all those roles we have played long enough. Sometimes we have belabored the point until we have become the very drama we've tried to avoid.

If you look up "who" and "what" in Webster's New Universal

Unabridged Dictionary, you will find that "who" refers to roles we play. Roles we play are the ego's way of shifting the attention from the Truth of what we are to a game of role-playing, none of which is real at all. One unfortunate aspect of role-playing is that as we give ourselves to those roles with all we are, we take our identity from them. Unfortunately, all too often we become hopelessly attached to them. Roles we play are not what we are, nor where we find our real identity. Our real identity is not found in some belief called a role, but rather only in the Truth of our Being.

To make matters even worse, making our living out of role-playing sets us up for being judged as to how well we are fulfilling each role. This puts the attention on the judgmental nature of ego consciousness rather than the simple discernment applied to how true we are to what we are. By discernment I mean that spiritual Truth is validated through simple comprehension of whether or not one is expressing conscious awareness of one's Truth. This plays out by the means validating the ends; each of our actions validates the end of expressing our divinity. This contrasts with what we find by exercising one's ego consciousness through judgmental application—that which divides and keeps us separate one from another by believing that the ends justify the means.

This may well explain why so many of us feel such deep emotional turbulence during the transitions between the many roles we play. We have attached our identity to a moving target, one false belief after another. When the roles shift we tend to think we have lost our identity, because the role is gone and so must our identity have faded with it. We are not only afraid we have lost our identity, but in more dramatic cases like retirement, for example, we feel like we are about to die. In a spiritual sense, this is true. A false image, a former idol, a falsely placed attachment to an identity affixed to a role dies to the Truth of the matter. When we give no power to role-playing we are born again to Truth, our only real identity.

It is this "born again" nature that I call awareness, the spiritual acknowledgment of the voice of the Christ we are led to express. It is heroic to allow oneself to become aware of the Wisdom in our midst and then to live by it, and it alone. Remember this: there is nothing opposed to the voice heard in silence, and thus nothing we need to choose over some figment of illusion. Truth just is and needs only to be lived, to Be. "To Be or not to Be? This is the question."

If our belief in duality and its relentless penchant for roles as a vehicle for identification is what we're living in any given moment, who or what is it we really are? And what, therefore, is our real identity?

Again, from the same dictionary source, the term "what" refers to the essence of God, divine consciousness. That is our essential Being—and our only real identity. This true identity can never change, no matter how we behave on a day-to-day basis. Identity is very much like character: we don't need to develop either. Life merely reveals them to us. Each is already present, awaiting only our awareness and expression. Life provides the opportunity for doing so.

After all this time, we finally come to realize the Truth: we are not a "who" at all, but rather a "what." This sounds impersonal, I know, but that does not change the Truth finally found. "What," being the essence of God—Wisdom waiting to be personified—is what informs our meaning and purpose. And it foresees its manifestation out into the world. What could be more beautiful and complete?

In this regard, it will do us well to recall Jesus' admonition, "I knew your name before you were born." What could that possibly mean? When viewing this declaration spiritually we are able to discern that before we were born into duality we were called something other than human. What might that be? Go within—give it no thought. Obviously, I cannot gnow or list your responses here; only you can fathom the Truth for you. What came up for me was the name, divine. Why not? After all, we call a newborn baby divine. We label our new lover divine. We even give testimony to some culinary orgasm as simply divine.

However, there is even a precursor to divine. It is each " inspirational idea." Yes, idea. Every spiritual demonstration begins with inspiration, a divine idea that activates it into Being. Just do not take divine into the world of duality by saying that for "divine" to exist as an idea what is not divine must also exist as a thought form or idea. That is the familiar dualistic argument against God being all. Do not go there. It is a delusional path that can only lead you astray. Such an idea is a distraction from spiritual reality, when inner spirit (inspiration) or idea is the only spiritual reality that activates demonstration out of Wisdom. Hence, our sole, and Soul, purpose of physical Being.

In this vein, is it easier to give up the idea that we are some personal entity, separate from the rest of the world and God, or instead accept and live the Truth that we are All That Is? We are formed in the image and likeness of the only personal One, yet infinitely individualized as you and me. Someone certainly could say that formed in another's image is hardly personal, yet in the spiritual world such judgments fail to exist. No such labels apply. If we persist in feeling that such a portrayal is impersonal, it is just the ego in us that is insisting on taking what is not personal, personally. Taking it personally is a sure sign that we are still under the illusory influence of ego consciousness.

To think that we are a separate, personal entity, and not akin to One, is the height of vanity. Vanity is the ego's prize weapon, used to combat our inner gnowing that we are One. It is the ego's way to have us reside in the warped consciousness that says we are individual personalities, a series of roles, playing as if they are what determine our identity. So forget any idea of having a "pity party" about thinking you are made from impersonal divine consciousness. How much more personal can we be formed than to have our Being demonstrated out of the One and only Being?

The terms or labels "impersonal" and "personal" do not really matter, anyhow. It is only when we are performing in ego consciousness that we need such labels. Once again, in spiritual consciousness such labels are nonexistent; all is One, and that is all that matters.

As we begin each moment with the Truth found in Wisdom, we come to Life from a rich foundation of what we really are instead of the false notions of who we are not. The question then becomes this: are you wed to the consciousness of divine essence, which comes only from within? Or are you wed to the reflection of the ego's view, which comes mostly from believing what so many have told us about "who" we are or ought to be? Then, of course, there is the huge influence of thousands of years of mass consciousness weighing on us. Yet most of us are not even aware of its existence, let alone of its huge influence when we are unaware of inner Truth.

Spiritually speaking, this is a definitive metaphysical declaration if I have ever heard one: Life is not about finding *who* you are; our existence is about expressing Life out of *what* we are! What we are is divine consciousness, essence, or divine idea; inspiration or Wisdom activated into demonstration. And it is always the Truth.

When lacking awareness, we are led to believe we are less than good enough. We are original sinners, and we are separate from God. Not so, not so, and absolutely not so! Nothing can take away the Truth of infinity, immortality, and eternal awareness. Not even if some church leader or holy writ seems to say so.

In The Inward Way, God and we are One. Each and all is that. Jesus said: "I and my Father are one." Of course, he did not mean that God was his biological father—or that his mother was irrelevant to his declaration, and that somehow they are joined at the hip. Rather, it is conscious awareness of Wisdom that regularly and faithfully parents our individualization of it, so the terms father and mother lack real meaning here. Saying that God creates all means that Wisdom, when understood and obeyed or followed, is that which demonstrates all like itSelf. This refers to all of us the same. Yes, all is like you and me in this Spiritual world—we are One. This is atonement—at-One-ment—demonstrated.

In the "I" of the beholder

To clarify, the "I" that is in "I am that, I am," (not I am that I am) is the one and only "I." This One "I" is the impersonal, grand, eternal, immortal, one and only and infinite "I" of all sentient beings. Yet this divine "I," or divine consciousness, is infinitely individualized. Think of the meaning of Jesus' declaration this way: "Whatever God is, I, also, Am That; I Am." This also makes all of us that; we are, truthfully. In the world of which Jesus spoke we truly are One in Being. Therefore, there is no grand "I," God, and a lot of little "i's," you and me. There is only one "I," and when we drop the error in our thinking that limits us to our "puny" selves, we begin manifesting as the One and only "I" we really are.

What is it this One and only "I" looks like? We cannot describe what God or divine inspiration looks like. Rather, inwardly, we *experience* God *as* the face of Wisdom. One way or another, I dare say each of us has experienced God as our innate Wisdom, that waits to inform as we become aware. When we more clearly understand our relation with God through experiencing Wisdom in the depths of our hearts, we come to comprehend that consciousness is all there is. Spiritually, then, we find ourselves to be and manifest no other Love, no other Wisdom or Truth, no other sense of Life—because this is all Life contains and is.

Now this is our real identity: the universal, divine, impersonal, one and only "I," the face experienced as Wisdom. God is that, you are that, and so am I. And the good news is that we can never lose what we really are. Not unlike the rest of the Universe, what we really are is the One Wisdom infinitely individualized.

The common error in our thinking is that we are so much less than the one "I" that we see ourselves manifesting mostly what is not of divine consciousness or from Wisdom's source at all. This is not the Truth. This feeling "less than" we really are, or even "less than" simply good enough, is an erroneous vision of Life. Trapped in this misunderstanding of Life and our part in it, we feel compelled to work extra hard just to gain Life's approval and feel we have some individual worth. This is a sure sign we have trapped ourselves in the illusory world of ego.

The Truth is that most of us, most of the time, are exhibiting or demonstrating divine consciousness. The self-perceived so-called errors in our behavior consist only of a relatively minor distancing from our Truth. This is caused by our belief in the absence of eternal Wisdom rather than acknowledging it as our only Truth of Being. Said another way, we're temporarily exhibiting an erroneous belief in the absence of God. Or, when we behave in some untoward fashion, it could simply be that we've temporarily forgotten what we really are. That is largely because we have been influenced by the historical belief in collective consciousness, the belief in being separate from some God on high, whom we cannot ever please because of our sinful nature. In a word, this is sheer nonsense!

We can benefit mightily from exploring the forgotten principles that make Life real. Jesus lived in the framework of Spirit, and thus beckoned all who would follow his way to do the very same. Even as powerful as his vision was, John the Baptist saw God and all else; he saw man as beneath, and separate from, God. He couldn't carry Jesus' sandals, it has been said; meaning that he could not walk in Jesus' shoes, that is, fully fathom his way of Being. Spiritually, what Jesus saw—the *only* thing he saw—was the embodiment of all as divine essence, with nothing to change or heal. Truly, Jesus was a master metaphysician; in his mind duality did not exist. Wisdom, or the Christ, was the only reality that fed his Life.

Just remember that in a metaphysical sense, it is not healing that is taking place. Instead, it is a shift in meaning we are giving Life, and thus holding the spaciousness for all others to be entranced in this same self-fulfilling grace. It is in this grace that our pain and afflictions disappear from view. And we see Life anew.

Using the ego for good

Some think we need to get rid of our ego in order to be spiritual. Not so. Spiritually, the appearance of ego or the small self can be helpful. The varied expressions of a belief in ego consciousness can provide more than ample testimony to a belief in the separation from God, or spiritual consciousness. "Well, then, how can this be helpful?" you might ask.

The ego can be helpful, just like the large feathery cobwebs on the long, wood-plank bridge I travel over on my meditative walk every other day. We can refer to them in several ways. Are they scary and dangerous, or simply metaphors for the ways we can feel or get trapped and devoured by illusion, the rational lies we have been led to believe are Truth? The cobwebs can be seen as part of Life's simple beauty, especially when backlit, that is, when seen as a glorious spiritual gift to the planet. Seen with disfavor, they tell us that on the illusory plane of ego consciousness there are material traps that can trip us up. However, when we are more aware, we can avoid those illusory traps by staying on our real path of Truth expressed. We just stand tall and walk in our Truth, right past the illusions we erroneously think can pull us down or trap us. What we see or project outside on our screen of Life is the mere representation of our current level of consciousness. It is an image depicting a direct relation between how we are seeing our divinity and its expression.

In the absence of this understanding we find it easy to see faults and errors in and by others. Yet, when we are troubled by what we are seeing, it is sure evidence that we are in some fashion denying these very same characteristics in ourselves. If you see someone abusing another, for example, and the abuse bothers you a good deal, this could well mean that somehow you are abusive toward yourself. Of course, we would naturally want to stop the abuse, and should.

If the abuse is against us, and we tolerate it, we can be assured that we are being abusive in at least two ways. First, we are being abusive toward ourselves for allowing the abuse to continue toward us. We also are being abusive toward the abuser, for to allow the other to abuse holds them in self-contempt, guilt, and shame—and perhaps prophesizes a future jail sentence. By enabling, we thus become the real abuser, often out of a false sense of compassion. Real compassion, like everything else, begins at home, within. When we come to a view of Life that begins in the seat of Wisdom, we treat ourselves with compassion out of loyalty to the Truth.

If we observe an effect in material life that does not match spiritual consciousness, like seeing someone being rude or manipulative, we can take it simply as a sign that we still believe we are separated from divine consciousness. That is not the Truth, but dressed in the gown of duality that is how we are seeing and expressing it. Seen instead in a newfound awareness, we change our perception back to the original, true form: from ego consciousness or duality back to spiritual consciousness. In this way, various appearances of ego consciousness, whether they are our own or expressed by another, regularly inform us of yet another opportunity to become aware of what we really are. This is where our character shows up, validating our change in behavior.

When we see God or Wisdom not *in*, but *as* One and all, we also come to respect the dignity of it all. There are no real differences when we see all of Life as divine essence. We are all the same—not identical, mind you—because each of us and every thing is a divine individualization of that essential essence of Being.

The divine nature found in Wisdom is the essential element of Life. How Wisdom is formed constitutes the individuation and individualization of the common Truth each of us is. What we now seem to be is the outward manifestation of our current state of divine awareness. Thus all one need do to find out what that state is, is to look in the mirror called Life and view it, unattached to its outcome. In this way we step away from the judgmental nature of ego consciousness and accept what we see with the fullness of compassion we deserve.

Now we are able to see how various expressions of ego consciousness can inform and point us to the Truth. We all know Truth when we see it: we see the Truth with our spiritual eyes— through intuition and insight. And the darkness of ignorance turns into light via deeper meaning, through enlightenment.

Here is the "be-all, end-all" of the matter. In the Prologue to the Gospel of John we are told, "In the beginning was the Word; the Word was with God, and the Word is God." The Word, as we now gnow, is the awareness of Wisdom waiting to be expressed. Being aware of Truth and living from it brings this consciousness into the world on every plane of existence. It is our Being. It is divine consciousness found in Wisdom that leads us eternally through Life, as the highest good for one and all.

Seen from this perspective, then, what the Gospel of John is saying to us is that at the initiation of any manifestation of Truth is the awareness of eternal Wisdom, that which ushers Truth across the threshold of Life. It follows—just as divine or First (the only) cause is inseparable from its effect—that Wisdom is *with* God because Wisdom *is* God. It is from such grace that we finally come to know what "I" is. Truly, I Am that—and so are you that:

Wisdom individualized and individuated. Truly, when you become aware of *what* you really are, you'll be what you really want to see.

Chapter Four

Principle 2: Being and staying in your spiritual awareness determines what is real

> "Tao is the Tao that is not spoken....
> Listen to it, but you cannot hear it!
> Its name is 'Soundless.'"
> Lao Tze

This second principle comes out of what we have forgotten about Life. And how I arrived at my favorite spiritual story. I will explain that this way.

Spiritual awareness as prophesying

I love to shop, not for the shopping itself but for what usually happens at the check-out counters. Sound strange? Perhaps this explanation will clear it up. When checking out at a grocery store, the attendant will usually ask: "How are you?" Inwardly, I smile immediately at the prospect. My response is a quick: "I am just perfect," and then I pause to see what their response is. If none, I will then add: "Just like you are." That usually gets them. Either they get the point immediately or they go into complete denial of their perfection. If they respond with denial, like, "No, not me; I am far from perfect," I then rejoin with: "Oh, have you forgotten?" That phrase is the awakener, the one that almost all get; it puts them into remembrance with their divinity. In the overwhelmingly large proportion of cases this is so. Nothing more need be said to them. The point has been made—and owned.

Try this for yourself when you shop. Not only will it stun many back into their spiritual reality but it will also bolster the

Truth within you. This one act will help you to remember that you, too, always have been, are, and always will be—just perfect. Did Jesus not admonish us this way: "Be ye perfect, even as your father in Heaven is perfect?" Did he also not tell us that God, divine consciousness, "is the same yesterday, today and tomorrow?" You gnow now why this also is the Truth for you. You always have been, are, and always will be just perfect, just as God is perfect—precisely because you are One in Being—of the One and same divine essence.

Very few of these delightful servants ask what it was they forgot. To that I have said something about the divine perfection they witnessed at their entry into this plane. The conversation goes on from there, something like this: "You and I are created as perfect spiritual Beings, and nothing can change that perfect essence. That is all there really is, and that is eternally the Truth of Being. The only reason we do not think we are perfect is because we have taken others' ideas of us as the Truth, when they represent only their thoughts, beliefs and opinions. We also have taken on, quite predominantly, the collective view or mass consciousness about Life. Quite simply, this is placing faith in others' views rather than in Truth. In spiritual terms, faith thus placed is a losing proposition. It is a lie seeming to be true.

To continue, I would tell them that none of that changes what we are. No matter what happens to us on this plane, we remain spiritual Beings, divine essence, Wisdom, spiritual consciousness individualized, and thus are perfect. We are perfect whether we want to admit it or not, because we are nothing but what we really are; thoroughly, completely, perfectly, and only divine consciousness individualized, contrary to outer appearance. Just as an apple is that and a tree is that, you and I are that.

Undoing false reality

The perfection found in Wisdom lacks only our awareness and acceptance in order for it to be activated. I will say this again, just for reinforcement: all our perfection lacks is our awareness and acceptance. It is the combination of awareness and acceptance that activates Wisdom's perfection into Being on all planes of existence.

Speaking of planes of existence, in the Gospel of John Jesus told us that God is spiritual, and thus we must look at God and Life spiritually, that is, as an inspirational idea, an idea parented out of the womb of Wisdom. Life has shown me that we become spiritually aware—enlightened—through the eyes of intuition, insight, and metaphor, and not through the physical senses. Inspirational ideas come to us by abiding consciousness awareness, not from a belief in duality or ego consciousness. When we become aware of this deeper consciousness we also come to see that it is this very same consciousness that leads the way to spiritual transformation, if, indeed, not transcendence itself.

Thus we come to see the face of God—Wisdom's meaning for us. This way of seeing deals with Truth, and how Wisdom can and will play out once held in the faith of God. This is what it means for Truth to manifest only in its image—as the natural outcome of Wisdom in some material form. This inevitable outcome, through what is called the law of order, also casts away the dualistic concept of opposites, like health and illness, for example. The manifestation of Wisdom's inspiration just is what it is, and needs no other qualifiers for it to be that—nor any choice to be one or the other.

Once again, First Cause, as defined by Aristotle, refers to the one real cause of all spiritual demonstration. As we find in Webster's New Universal Unabridged Dictionary, this is what Aristotle meant by metaphysics. Not that metaphysics lacks the material, but rather that spiritual demonstration has order and it is conscious awareness of inspiration that activates its image and likeness into individualized form. The outcome is inseparable from its source, a spiritual idea in its foundation.

Whatever other viewpoint we take about spiritual demonstration is an illusion, made up by man in ego's image, as a way
of fulfilling ego's desire for us to be separate from God, the still,
small voice of Wisdom. This desire to be separate is duality
defined, and the height of vanity. The ego is very clever in this
regard, knowing that the same law or dynamic works for ego
consciousness as it does for divine consciousness. There is one
major difference, however: ego consciousness cannot manifest
anything spiritual, cannot demonstrate Wisdom; it can muster
only some clever idea formed out of self-important desire. On the
other hand, divine consciousness manifests only the highest
good — the *only* good, I should say — for all concerned.

Perhaps a simple example will illustrate Aristotle's view. We
look at a table fashioned out of wood and we call it, simply, a
table. We might embellish that some by calling it a beautiful
table, but usually we just casually refer to it as a table. The label
takes on our view of outer appearance, the table, rather than
focusing on the Wisdom from which inspiration flows into
material reality.

"Well," you might say, "if this is the case, then let us back up
a bit and say that this table in front of us is really a tree, fashioned
or formed into a beautiful table." You would certainly be on the
right track with such a declaration. And I suspect a good wood-
worker would agree with you. But a master wood-worker would
gnow there is so much more to and in a table than this limited
perception would permit. The master craftsman, by the
connection he makes with the wood and the tree, is able to spiritually discern its fiber to be the essence of God that made the tree
possible in the first place. His connection with divine essence is
that profound and that deep. This is what makes him a master —
and what gives his demonstrations Soul.

If we trace the table back to its source properly, then we will
come to see that the table is God, divine essence or inspiration
manifested in significantly individualized expressions of

awareness along the way. The first or only cause is what has been parented, brought to Life—in this case through two iterations of inspiration demonstrated into material form, ending up, finally—you guessed it—as the table. This is a good thing to remember about all of Life, for real Life reflects this same heritage and none other.

Let us remember this, too, about first cause—it is not the roles we play, but only our Truth in which we walk that determines our identity. As we practice staying in awareness of our divine essence, it has us expressing our divinity at every level: we act from it, and thus we are actually Being it. So forget not, remember always: practice, practice, and practice some more—practice staying aware of inspiration's voice.

Actually, it is this awareness that declares spiritual intimacy. Intimacy is not some feeling we have about our relationship with another. And it is not about sharing our deepest secrets with another. Nor is it the height of physical intimacy shared during passionate sexual activity. Authentic intimacy begins with an awareness of our divinity. Once that is accepted, it filters through to every level of Life. Intimacy is then felt in all aspects of personal engagement. We come to feel intimate even with plants and animals, just as we do in our relationships with all who come into our path. The key, however, is becoming intimate first with our awareness of what we truly are, being intimate with the inner voice we hear and expressing it thus. It is the only real cause of anything that follows on a relational level.

I am reminded of the marvelous introduction to the movie, "Crash," where, in the opening scene, one of the main characters says something like this: "We are so hardened and numbed that we keep crashing into one another just so we can feel something on some level." We keep forgetting that we are not separate, but One. Distractions that stem from a belief in ego and mass consciousness are frequent and often disabling. This is a powerful warning to which we might well pay attention.

Distraction is yet another means of keeping us behind the veil that separates us from our Truth. Communing with Truth defines spiritual intimacy, which renders Life authentic for us.

The pathway to spiritual meaning

We find Truth, the deeper meaning lodged in Wisdom, neither in books nor in voices. By looking within, we are able to see beyond the messenger to the message, to the voice of inner Authority. To reinforce this point, it is neither our intellect nor our senses—like eyes, ears, and brain—from which we get spiritual Truth. These are really only metaphors for the spiritual senses: intuition, insight, meaning, comprehension, enlightenment, transformation, transcendence, and resurrection. In a very real way, our inner senses serve us more deeply than we normally think of them doing, not physically, but metaphorically.

For example, when we say, "Oh, now I see what you mean," as a metaphor we do not mean we saw something with our physical eyes. Instead, we came to a deeper comprehension of what was being said, from whence spiritual meaning emanates. We also say, "Oh, now I hear you," meaning essentially the same as "seeing it;" we have gained a new perspective on some issue, concern, or idea. Likewise, we "taste the bitterness" of an argument or in defeat; and we are "touched" by a sensitive note from a dear friend. These examples speak to spiritual Truth and not physicality at all. In this sense is the only real spiritual meaning found. Our physical senses cannot, in and of themselves, do anything like hear, see, or taste on a spiritual level—but physical senses *can* serve as metaphors to help us experience a deeper sense of Life.

Coming to gnow the Truth in this fashion makes us free; gives us permission, if you will, to live it. Otherwise we succumb to beliefs about ourselves, others, and Life in general that really are untruths, errors, or illusions, and we are imprisoned by them. The familiar admonition to "know thyself" speaks to this very point.

"Gnowing thyself" validates the Scriptural reference that we come to know as we are known. Now, however, we have come to comprehend the fullest meaning, that we gnow as we are gnown, from the power exhibited only from the Truth we find and live from within. When we gnow thy Self, that is, when we are in touch with our Truth, then we, without question or doubt, demonstrate that exact image and likeness. It will not necessarily be in the same form, but it will be clearly identifiable as its first and only cause, nonetheless. If, for example, I see myself as whole and complete, I will not seek elsewhere for someone to complete me and make me whole.

In the final analysis, it is not the Truth that makes us free. It is the *gnowing* of the Truth that makes us free—both to Be the Truth, as well as demonstrating it faithfully. It is experiencing the Truth *as* Truth that does the setting free, free from all the old habits of belief and opinion that simply cannot work in the spiritual world. Such illusions are nothing but duality portrayed.

This setting free leads us to a clear and meaningful spiritual definition of forgiveness. Forgiveness is about giving up all those insidious beliefs, opinions, and roles that, in the physical world, we have taken to be the Truth for us and, instead, moving on to the only real Truth. This elevates the cheap, superficial form of forgiveness to the single act that frees one and all from the ill-effects of guilt and shame that come with taking others' acts and expressions personally. Shifting our perspective on Life from the unreal to Truth is what forgiveness is about, at the least for we who hold ourselves responsible for forgiving others. Coming to the spiritual perspective is forgiveness personified.

I like to wear what has become my favorite T-shirt, the one that says on the front: LOVE OUT LOUD! The spiritual Truth is that we do not need words or songs that come out of our mouths to express love out loud, not at all. Loving out loud is more about how we express what we really are, not about words. It's about being True to the voice of Wisdom and only that. Thomas Keating, a Trappist contemplative monk, tells us that silence is the language God speaks, and all else is a mistranslation. Indeed, it is out of silence that loving out loud is made manifest.

Words themselves can only point to Truth, but Truth itself emanates only from Wisdom heard in silence: silence heard between words when we listen carefully; silence heard between the lines when we read from a focus on inner meaning; the silence we hear in the wind's whisper, "I love you," as it busses our cheek on a warm summer eve at sunset; the silence we feel by quieting our own beliefs and opinions in favor of the Truth our hearts speak. In each example of silence we hear inspiration speaking to us as Wisdom. As we get ourselves there, to the vacuum created out of silencing our beliefs and opinions nestled in some form of fear, we can rest assured that, when there, inspiration will do her job faithfully and righteously.

When we silence all forms of ego consciousness, it is there where we hear the immortal, all-powerful voice speak: "Be still and know I am God." And, "I am that, I am," meaning divine consciousness, Wisdom, the Truth of our Being is that. Yes, the voice we hear within is that which Loves out loud. It is the beginning and the end, all as One. All else is a mistranslation we take for the Truth.

Spiritual meaning is not about opinion formed from the ego conscious elements of intellect and linear rationality, but is discerned through an inner experience of authentic gnowing. Intuition is Truth understood, Wisdom heard. Indeed, intuitive impressions are received through the silence that speaks only Truth to us. Thus intuition and spiritual meaning are inseparable. One is the reflection of the other. And metaphor informs the process.

The spiritual context for belief and opinion

Speaking about opinion, there is a story about a group having a business meeting in order to arrive at some strategic decisions. As the discussion progressed, everyone but Mary were giving their opinions. They were scattered all over the topic, some good and others lukewarm. Finally, someone noticed that Mary had not yet contributed to the discussion and said: "Mary, what's your opinion about all this? You've been quiet today." "Oh," Mary responded reflectively, "I was just being silent so I could hear the Truth of the matter." Point well made. Learning to reconnect with Life on this level is a gift to be treasured—and to be used for the utmost good of all concerned.

Beliefs we hold sacred are but collective consciousness and ego consciousness operating to hold us in place—the place of limitation instead of the boundless capacity or limitless realm of possibility. Holding on to a particular belief helps manifest in material form the content and intention of that belief. The only difficulty is that such manifestations come out of illusory configurations of reality. If one holds on to material as the reality, then this is precisely the type of belief that perpetrates the ego consciousness belief in life and death. Why would we ask so little out of Life, unless we believed that Life were this limited, this small? Dare we see God, and thus ourselves, as bigger than the limitations we often put on both? Dare we see that Life, real Life, is All, formed only out of spiritual consciousness?

Life is about seeing from the macro plane, not the micro plane. The latter can be somewhat helpful, but it also is limiting, just like beliefs are. Besides, opposition can always be found to one belief or another. Duality is thus perpetuated through belief. Only the experience of gnowing our inner resonance with the Truth is the answer. When Truth shows its face, it eliminates duality in a single stroke of genius. Do not confuse belief or opinion with the Truth if you really want only the Truth.

Mary Baker Eddy said this about Jesus: "His teaching set households at variance, and brought to material beliefs not peace, but a sword." What a vibrant testimony to the process of cutting away the conviction of material belief! Let this be an admonition we never forget. We must view Life as a perpetual opportunity to cut away erroneous belief, and in its place install only what we come to gnow as Truth by experiencing it inwardly. It is the difference between night and day, between ignorance and the Truth found in spiritual enlightenment.

Spiritually, we cannot make this physical existence a better place because this *isn't* the *real* place. It is only the result of a delusional thought system; mass consciousness infused and expressed. It took mass consciousness for Hitler to overrun Europe and crucify the Jews. It has taken the mass consciousness of fear to initiate and perpetuate the war in Iraq and elsewhere. It takes mass consciousness to maintain the extraordinary level of poverty and environmental destruction we have on this planet. Likewise, it has taken a belief in mass consciousness to establish and maintain our focus on duality over spiritual reality. If we are aware we need not count the ways; they are all too evident in the midst of us.

A needless striving for peace

As we bring these disrupting factors into view we can see that they distract us from experiencing the inherent peace that is found in the conscious awareness of Wisdom. We cannot find real, lasting peace somewhere "out there," through barter and advocacy. We can only bring ourselves into the conscious awareness of the peace we already are and demonstrate that. As each of us becomes aware of the peace we are—instead of the dis-ease we feel much of the time—that deep, penetrating feeling of ease energizes every cell of our bodies, and we are renewed throughout. Acknowledging what we are brings ultimate reality to the fore, and the feeling of serenity along with it. The feeling of serenity reveals the shift in Life's purpose gained from the true meaning of our essence now remembered.

Healing is about turning over a new leaf, exercising a new

way of viewing Life; one that relieves the stress caused by living a lie encapsulated in error. It is not a physical happening at all. Rather than a healing that has taken place, it is an awareness of our highest good reappearing to us. Therefore, as we begin to live again from divine consciousness, the stress also leaves our earthly consciousness. When this happens, our physical bodies begin to act on the new messages as they eavesdrop on all we gnow and express. All the rest that is good is bound to follow; is given unto us.

Remember, what we are Being in our hearts is what we really want out in the world beyond. That is the image to faithfully abide. Loving what we are with *all* we are—through our constant awareness of this Truth—is what restores us to peace. Peace thus becomes a part of all the rest that is added unto us. That is the promise we find in Jesus' teachings: inner peace felt in the only moment there is, the eternal now.

When we view the process of spiritual fulfillment, we come to see we have moved away from a very immature belief in a kind of peace for which we barter endlessly. We move to a more expansive perspective in which we Be the peace we want to see, rather than engaging the victimized perspective where others and particular situations seem to rob us of peace.

As we continue into the expansiveness of divine consciousness, we soon become aware that we have, at last, found our home. That home is you, and me, and all like us, with all the attributes and characteristics of that entity we have called God. Now we gnow we are the consciousness which demonstrates peace, love, patience, compassion, and happiness. Thus we come to feel at home, and peace prevails without any effort from us at all.

Being happiness

Because of the mass consciousness that feeds this material life, many of us take on the belief that material means can meet spiritual need, like happiness. This can never be the Truth. The material can never fulfill the spiritual need, can really never make us happy. Besides, happiness, like peace, is an inherent characteristic of spiritual life, not found in the material.

For example, having more personal wealth can never make us happy or bring us real peace of mind. Nor can it really make us feel secure and prosperous, or free from bondage. More personal wealth can make us feel temporarily giddy and materially satisfied. It also can falsely make us think we're secure and prosperous one moment—and in the next we fear that what wealth we have will not really be enough, or won't last, or could be taken away from us. In this scenario we do not have peace of mind, either. Nor are we free from the tethers of other fear-related thoughts.

However, when we come to comprehend that our natural state is being happy, this also brings with it peace of mind and a joy-filled heart. When we are secure in our divinity, we come to gnow ourselves as happiness righteously expressed. The Kingdom is ours to have and hold—and, therefore, to manifest. The spiritual can always meet the needs of the material. It is only in the security of our Truth that we come to fulfillment in all other ways. The list of the ways in which we are fulfilled is endless, as is the promise of the Kingdom. The Kingdom of inspiration—the infinitude of Wisdom—is infinite and immortal in its promise for us. Fear not. Knock at the door of your real freedom and prosperity. Your Truth awaits you. Your Truth *is* you, the one and only *real* you.

You are the gift

Each of us has had at least a glimpse of divine revelation or consciousness that has awakened us to some amazing possibility for us—some new, even deeper meaning for us. Yet, for the most part—largely because of earthly pressures or the impact of those naysayers in our lives—we let that glimpse fall from view, and from memory. Here is the good news: because we *are* divine, spiritual consciousness is always with us. All it takes is some simple realization or recollection—awareness, if you will—that it is present, and we can begin again with what we have found there, as if we had never left it behind. As though no time has passed since we first heard Truth's calling. Actually, no real time *has* passed, since time is an ego configuration, not a spiritual one. Real Life is expressed in each ever-present moment, so it's always time to begin anew from the basis of the individualized Truth for us. After all is said and done, yesterday is history. Tomorrow is mystery. Today is a gift. That is why we call it "the present." Why not live the present in celebration of this Truth?

Indeed, there is no time like the present. There is *only* the present, the gift we can celebrate moment by moment. "Now" is a never-ending eternity. All of us can recall times when we lost ourselves in some creative act that ended with the innocent query, "Goodness, where did the time go?" It is our investment in the "now" that establishes eternity as the only reality. What a marvelous gift this is, freeing us from the boundary of linear time and all the stress that comes with it. Living each eternal moment of "now" is a celebration of the gift it is, the present simply being what is intended to be, eternally so. A friend tells about a participant in a seminar he was attending having removed the hands from her watch, and replacing the crystal with one that had embossed on it the word: now. Whenever someone asked her what time it was, she would look at her watch and respond with a gnowing smile, "It's now."

What I am talking about here is the promise of spiritual Life: whatever inspiration brings to us is to be expressed, and now. It is said in Scripture: "Whatever you do to the least of my brothers, you do unto me." Symbolically this admonition has nothing to do with our relations with others. Metaphorically, this Scriptural reference means that each divine idea, each gift of inspiration— no matter how large or how small each image might seem—is of equal importance, simply because each is divine. Neither size nor the appearance of relative importance should carry any weight with us. Each divine idea—each child borne out of the womb of Wisdom—awaits only our acknowledgment of it, and our unfailing surrender and commitment to it, in each moment of now we have. To love what we are with all our heart, soul, and strength commits to it the faith of God.

Aristotle brilliantly conceived the absolute and only cause, and determined it to be inseparable from like effect. Like begets like. Therefore we can never say it is too late. Or that one divine idea or another is too small, or seemingly unimportant. Nor can what is given unto us ever fail when we commit all we are to it. It is too late and can fail only if we fail in understanding this Truth about spiritual Life. Fail not. Re-member with your Truth, always—and the rest is given unto you.

When we become aware of our divine essence we come to see only Oneness, and in that Oneness our spiritual eyes are opened to see that there is neither illness nor health, neither gay nor straight, skin that is neither black nor white, red or yellow. In the world as Spirit, none of these exist, for there is no need for such distinctions when all of us are the One real "I". Therefore, we have no need for labels to make us real, or to acknowledge that Truth. Life just is; no labels attached.

On angels and miracles

It is as we live the Truth of divine consciousness that we see miracle after miracle appearing before our inner vision. In the framework of ego consciousness we get only an occasional glimpse of miracles in the outer world, and it usually takes a fairly large one to get our attention. However, when we are viewing Life like an eagle high on a cliff-side perch, we are able to see more of Life, and from a very different perspective. When viewing Life from a high degree of awareness, spirituality regularly informs us with the gifts of the Kingdom—and Life abounds with miraculous imagery. Indeed, our lives are filled with new intuitional and insightful presents.

I would not say the miracles become commonplace, because that could be understood to mean that we may one day take them for granted. Instead, the meaning of commonplace I would like to convey is that the beauty and form of spiritual miracles can be everywhere found as we go throughout our days and nights. When we see through our newfound spiritual eyes, Life in all its forms is miraculous to us. We no longer identify Life as mundane. Rather, we come to celebrate the divine, miraculous nature of which the mundane is composed. What could be better—and more the Truth? How miraculous!

This is somewhat like being able to see, and be informed by, angels. From a metaphysical point of view, angels are simply messages of Truth released from within, resonating as a sure path for us. From time to time we hear someone say something that moves us to Truth. Or it saves us from some kind of impending disaster. An angelic message can come to us as a book that seemingly jumps off the shelf into our hands. When opened at random, it has just the answer we need right then. I have heard it said that angels and miracles, and even coincidental happenings, are God's way of remaining anonymous. What is really happening is that we are put in touch with the calling of Soul—our own highest good, the Christ or Truth—so we can surrender to that voice rather than to some erroneous calling from outside us. This is a nice way of saying we have thus avoided the perils of duality.

In this way, we are touched by the voice of an angel that has only our best interest at heart. As we become more and more adept at listening for the voice of Spirit, we hear these angelic messages more regularly. As we surrender to the messages we hear, they become more prominent in our presence. From this presence we are born again to conscious awareness of inner Truth and live it faithfully.

We also hear angels speak when we listen carefully to the spaces between the words of a conversation with another; when we see the Truth spoken between the lines of elegant prose or idyllic poetic expressions; when we celebrate the sparkle of early morning dew on blades of grass; or simply when we are inspired by a suggestion that occurs to us "out of the blue." Agreed, these could well be slightly different renditions of what angels are, but when living in the world of divine consciousness things just look and sound very different from what we're used to seeing and hearing.

When you are able to view Life from such a perspective, not only will your Life be filled with angels all around you, but you will also come to see that you, too, are angelic. Others will surely see you this way; perhaps already do, even though they might not call you by that name. They might just say that they find you immensely helpful or inspirational, or that you lift their spirits. Either way, your behavior fits the description of One. At first you might feel overcome with such a spiritual idea, but the Truth never hurts. It only informs us what it is. So get used to it, already! That's when the miracles really show up.

Ego's indifference to awareness

When using spiritual vision we welcome awareness of our inner perspective. As Shakespeare said, "Let every eye negotiate for itself, and trust no agent"—simply brilliant in its spiritual conveyance. Do we go to our inner Authority or some outer one for information, approval, and validation? We can ask someone else what is good or right for us, but that answer will not necessarily be the one that fits us. Only we can really gnow the Truth of our Being. Where, then, do we find authenticity, our real meaning and purpose?

I am sure you will recall the story about Jesus in the synagogue; how he turned the tables on the moneychangers and threw them out of the temple. In a spiritual context, this is a story that asks: "What is the legitimate currency of Life: spirituality, or sensuality and materialism; inner or outer authority? Which is the actual reality? Is it found in Truth or in duality? In Wisdom or in the illusions of the material world?"

Just gnow that when you make a choice you must reject anything and everything that is not that choice, or it will nag you endlessly with feelings of doubt, fear's uncomely cousin. When residing in the power of Wisdom, surrendering to the inherent Truth we feel there replaces the notion of choice. Such surrender is necessary if we are to establish our Life's real direction. Found in that surrender is the only real currency—that which will not only serve our highest good but also the highest and best for the Universe.

Jesus stood strong for the single way of spirituality instead of the false choices that occupy duality. He loved and stood for divine consciousness with all he was. How can we do less? "Give to Caesar what is Caesar's and to God what is God's," Jesus said to us. Given the current context, it might well be said: "Give to Caesar what is material; give to the spiritual world your spiritual awareness." For those whose consciousness is grounded in the material world, materiality is the vehicle of existence, and filled with choices galore. Contrarily, when we come to gnow there really is nothing *but* spiritual consciousness, we simply and faithfully express the One and only gift real Life is.

The Master Metaphysician also told us: "Greater is he that is in you, than he that is in the world." Metaphorically, Jesus was saying, "Greater is the divine consciousness you have within, than the materialistic renderings found in the world of ego consciousness."

What did Jesus mean when he told us, "I am the way, the truth and life?" Did he mean his own personal "I?" That Jesus, personally, is the way, the truth and life? Hardly. The real (spiritual) meaning of the "I" of which Jesus spoke is the One and only "I" we each are: the way of divine awareness. Truly, adhering to the whispers of Wisdom is the way, the Truth and Life—the One, in and as, all. Christ is the awareness and activity of the divine consciousness that speaks regularly through us as the Word of Wisdom. Therefore, we need not wait for the illusory return of Jesus at some future date before we are "saved." Wisdom saves us from our puny view of self each moment we are aware of its presence. Thus, we are the outward expression of the inward Truth of Wisdom, also called the Christ.

Jim Chasen, a poet and shaman friend who writes under the moniker, The Silent Lotus, says this about the voice we hear within: "May your voice be loving enough to silence your own fear." In this case, the fear speaks to the unbelief in the omnipresence of Wisdom. Such unbelief places us in a world of separation from our real identity, and the fear is that we will one day be all alone. Or, worse yet, that when we leave the physical body behind, we will cease to exist at all. The real voice of spiritual awareness, however, does indeed silence the fear elevated by belief in duality.

When we finally come to our resting place—our real home as it were—we will fully understand that our at-One-ment is eternal, immortal and infinite, and thus omnipotent, omniscient, omnipresent, and ever active. Ah, we are home at last, and forever so. And being and staying in the home of our spiritual awareness determines what is real.

Chapter Five

Principle 3: Divine creation is the result of Truth activated

"Not known, because not looked for
But heard, half-heard, in the stillness
Between two waves of the sea.
Quick now, here, now, always—
A condition of complete simplicity
(costing not less than everything.)"
T. S. Elliott

Whether we are conscious of it or not, some kind of creation is always happening. The creative principle of the universe is that the Mind, or spiritual consciousness, is your Mind, your consciousness—and my Mind, my consciousness. Divine awareness is infinite, and we are called, endlessly, to demonstrate it. Such consciousness is not a personal thing that you and I have, that is different from one another. What is different is intellect, for so-called intellect is an ego consciousness dimension and therefore must be judged and calibrated—labeled, if you will. Divine awareness, spiritual consciousness, is the Truth of our being, Wisdom waiting to be heard—the Christ consciousness—and it is the only real, meaning spiritual, Truth. In ego consciousness, the Truth of which we speak here is nonexistent. The only place Truth can be found is in our spiritual essence. As my wise father used to say: "You don't find a pear under an apple tree." Nor do you find Truth in the ego's den of iniquity—our falsely placed belief in a dream thought to be real.

It is good to be grounded in the difference between the two processes. Ego uses projection as its way. It projects error out onto our screen of dreams. When we're living out of ego consciousness, we believe what we see in the outer world is the Truth. When we find ourselves choosing one way or the other as our life path, this is the sure sign we are lodged in ego consciousness. In contrast, when we find ourselves living through intuition and insight, we can be sure this is only highest good extended on our behalf.

So, if we are to demonstrate the inward calling, how do we start? With what does spiritual demonstration begin? Well, we stop, we look, and we listen. How? When? Where? By residing in our hearts. "Go into your closet and pray," said Jesus, meaning metaphysically, "go within to where prayer is found, as a secret, and close the door behind you." This subtle difference in rendering is a powerful one, for it tips the metaphysical hand, in that we begin to see that prayer is not something we do, but something we find when we listen. Just what is it we find? We find that we are prayer manifested. How can this be? By listening within, in our hearts, from there and there alone the voice of Truth or the Christ consciousness comes, and we come to know that all is One. The secret we find within us, lodged in Wisdom, is that we are divine, and intuition releases this Truth to us time and time again. We hear it only when consciously aware.

Layers of illusory approach

Let us take a moment or two to look at how we think humanly, in contrast to how spiritual Truth emanates. The first level of thinking is what we might call personal. It comes from the idea that we have a life separate from God, Wisdom. Such a mental configuration says that in our separateness it is our job to think our way through Life, instead of letting Wisdom or consciousness awareness do its business, have its way with us. This is the ultimate duality: the call for outer signs versus The Inward Way. "I feel separate from God, therefore I must do this thing called life by myself." At its base is the false belief that we can do better than God; we want better than perfect. Funny, in Scripture we see that God only wanted to create, and he called it all good. We are not satisfied with simply letting creation find its way; we want to change it all, including most everything and everyone around us.

In this personal way, we try, try, try, and think, think, think about a kind of physical or material life, trying to figure it out for ourselves, mostly to meet our belief in ego needs. This way uses linear, rational intellect, discounting the spiritual value of intuition and insight. In a personal sense, we say to a perplexing issue, "I will think about that." No, Jesus said: "Give it no thought." No thought! "All the thinking you can do will not add one cubit of good to your life," he clarified.

Personal thought is self-absorbed, egocentric: "I," "I," "I". This comes from our belief in the "small i," which we maintain until we grow to understand the "one and only I", the "I" of which we all are made. This also makes it impersonal. It is the small "i" we think we are, manifested as smallness in our thought and action, that makes us think the "I" is personal. And when someone says or does something that irritates us or pricks our conscience, we take it all the more personally. That is the ego-conscious way of keeping us separate from God and others.

Giving thought or sticking with thought is what holds emotional pain in its place. It is what holds adults to the description of cement: all mixed-up and hardened. Whenever we feel an emotion, have a deep feeling come up—for whatever reason, it matters not why—we give the spaciousness necessary to move that feeling through and out of us only when we do not think about any facet of it. To the contrary, when we keep thinking about the painful emotions that seem to be troubling us—wondering what is their source, why they're here at all, and what meaning their expression must have for us on a physical level—it is those very thoughts that keep us in the dis-ease of the emotion. It is as though the emotion were, in fact, us, instead of needing only to pass through us. Rehearsal of those thoughts harden them, give them power they do not, in and of themselves, have. Thus the key to freedom is to not *become* the emotional feeling, nor to make it something other than an energetic form that needs to be set free. When we remember to abide in this Truth, we are made free, the reasons notwithstanding.

When we give power to our emotions, we put into action belief in worry or fret. Actually, worry and fret hold your emotional pain in place, even if you are unaware of the nature of feeling in the first place. This is one reason why we occasionally feel trapped in our emotions. In the physical realm emotions are trapped by the thoughts that caused them. This holds them in place instead of allowing the freedom to be expressed and thus released. This description epitomizes ego consciousness as the theory and practice of the illusion it is.

Belief in ego consciousness is also about working hard until someone we want to care about us thinks we are good enough, so we finally can get what we think we deserve: a good view of us. Most of these thoughts come from the beliefs of others, as well as those thoughts and beliefs that have come to nest from mass consciousness, established over centuries. The reality is that responses have meaning for us only when we give them power to do so. In and of themselves, views of others have no power of their own.

Beneath the belief in that false power is the underlying miasma of fear. In this form, we often see ourselves as victims of Life's outcomes. As a result, we often cast our circumstance in a negative light (darkness, ignorance). "They did this to me," "Life is a bitch waiting to express itself," "We are born, we suffer, we die; life is such a waste." We bury ourselves in language that tells of lost opportunities, which, of course, only tells us that it is we who have cast our place and roles in darkness. "I wish I had said no to that," "I wish I had thought deeper, done this, accepted that, protected myself." On and on it goes.

Contrary to this view, Jesus said: "My Kingdom is not of this world." What did he mean? The Kingdom, the spiritual Kingdom, that is, has nothing to do with ego-based thoughts. It has to do only with letting the Truth come to us from within, and living obediently only to that. It means to let only Wisdom reign. After all, when we come to the awareness of Wisdom we see that nothing else exists, including the false "gift" of choice.

This takes us to the mental realm, where we engage ourselves in seeing something from a different perspective. We may break a leg and see its benefits rather than the inconvenience of the plaster cast that seems to hold us fast. We speak of Life in terms of gratitude rather than victimization. "I am so glad for my husband," "I am so glad I decided to do what I felt called to do." In both of those first two means of thought, we are really working at it. Still, we are trying to make something different out of a paltry form of life rather than simply letting real Life have its way with us. "My kingdom is not of this world," we hear echoed in our hearts yet again, until we come to grips with its meaning for us.

The following is a story found on the Internet, which illustrates the difference between the personal and mental realms quite nicely:

"A university professor challenged his students with this question. "Did God create everything that exists? A student bravely replied, "Yes, He did!" "God created everything?" the professor asked. "Yes, sir," the student replied. The professor answered, "If God created everything, then God created evil, since evil exists. And according to the principal that our works define who we are, then God is evil." The student became quiet before such an answer. The professor was quite pleased with himself, and boasted to the students that he had proven once more that the faith in God is a myth.

Another student raised his hand and said, "Can I ask you a

question, professor?" "Of course," replied the professor. The student stood up and asked: "Professor, does cold exist?" "What kind of question is this? Of course it exists. Have you never been cold?" The students snickered at the young man's question.

The young man replied, "In fact, sir, cold does not exist. According to the laws of physics, what we consider cold is, in reality, the absence of heat. Everybody or object is susceptible to study when it has or transmits energy. Absolute zero (-460 degrees F) is the total absence of heat. All matter becomes inert and incapable of reaction at that temperature. Cold does not exist. We have created this word to describe how we feel if we have no heat."

The student continued. "Professor, does darkness exist?" The professor responded, "Of course it does." The student replied, "Once again you are wrong, sir. Darkness does not exist either. Darkness is, in reality, the absence of light. We can study light, but not darkness. In fact, we can use Newton's prism to break white light into many colors and study the various wavelengths of each color. You cannot measure darkness. A simple ray of light can break into a world of darkness and illuminate it. How can you know how dark a certain space is? You measure the amount of light present. Isn't this correct? Darkness is a term used by man to describe what happens when there is no light present."

Finally, the young man asked the professor, "Sir, does evil exist?" Now uncertain, the professor responded, "Of course, as I have already said. We see it everyday. It is in the daily example of man's inhumanity to man. It is in the multitude of crime and violence everywhere in the world. These manifestations are nothing else but evil."

To this the student replied, "Evil does not exist, sir, or at least it does not exist unto itself. Evil is simply the absence of God. It is just like darkness and cold—a word that man has created to describe the absence of God. God did not create evil. Evil is not like faith, or love, that exist just as does light and heat. Evil is the result of what happens when man does not have God's love present in his heart. It's like the cold that comes when there is no heat, or the darkness that comes when there is no light."

The professor sat down.

The young student's name? Albert Einstein."

(Author unknown)

Although there is no way to be assured that this conversation actually took place, the story makes its point clearly and precisely. Here is another story that did take place. Of this I am sure, for I was present to witness it in my own heart and soul. And it is one that makes an excellent bridge between the personal and mental realms, and also leads nicely to the spiritual realm.

A few years ago I was visiting my cousin, Tasos, in Athens, Greece. After we had put his then 91-year-old mother to bed, we went over to his apartment for a nightcap. As we sat on his balcony overlooking the city several stories about his life unfolded, most of them containing a good bit of drama. As he finished I said something like: "Gee, Tasos, I guess my life is simpler than that, thank God." Then I did remember something I thought was worth sharing. "Oh, I forgot," I began. "You remember me mentioning my friend Richard, don't you?" He nodded affirmatively. "Well, he just got his sixth divorce." Tasos took a long, considered sip from his glass of cognac and said, "Isn't...that...wonderful!" he drew his response out. "What," I said, "didn't you hear me? He just had his sixth divorce." "Yes, I heard you," he responded sensitively, "and isn't it wonderful that six different women could have loved him enough to marry him." A new perspective had arrived with its characteristic thump of Truth. Wisdom had spoken once again.

But this is not the end of the story. The minute I landed back in the States I called Richard and told him the story. Stunned silence was his only reply, so much so that I thought he had hung up the phone. "Are you there?" I asked. Time was pregnant with pause. "Yes...I'm here," he responded. "I was just witnessing the huge release of guilt and shame I've carried since my first divorce, which has only multiplied exponentially over the years. What a gift this is for me," he said with utmost sincerity and gratitude. "I cannot tell you what this has done for me; I'm not even sure I can put it into words. I guess that doesn't really matter. The only thing that does matter is that this awakening has given me a new lease on life and I am ever-grateful to both Tasos and you." Awareness is Life-changing, is it not? Indeed, it is that. Now, let us follow this transition into the spiritual way of Life.

The third realm of consciousness, after the personal and mental, and the only real dimenstion, is the spiritual, wherein we gain the Truth of any matter simply by going within our hearts, so we can hear that still, small voice that is Truth for us. Deeper and deeper we go, exercising our inherent desire to fathom the only real container of Life, to find Life's real meaning in Wisdom—not for anyone but us. Yet this way is highly imper-sonal, for it is not for the puny "i" that Truth is spoken. It is the only Truth, the only "I" there is, speaking not just for one or more of us, but as the One in which we have—and are—the Way, the Truth and Life. We tend to think that we are to move from one level to the next, although there are some who do leap the infer-ential gap through a gift of grace. In the life of the ego, we think we can gain the Truth from some outside authority, some idol outside ourselves. Is there not Scripture that speaks to worshipping false idols? Well, this is the false idol of outer appearance, all these false idols we find in the life of the ego, various figments of beliefs and opinions we have taken for Truth. Now we gnow better, and we can manifest on a completely different level by setting the false idols aside, just as Jesus did.

If we apply this understanding to the story about my friend, Richard, above, we would see him going within for the Truth of the situation for him. In metaphysical terms we would want him to see that marriage has to do with his relationship with Self, the Truth of his Being. He would then be wed to The Inward Way. It is this to which he must remain faithful. It is about finding himself congruent with the voice of Wisdom. As he does, then he is really being faithful to Life individualized and thus finds himself completed in that rather than through some external validation. All his relationships would then be filled with the authenticity of the Loving Way, and guilt and shame would have no place to hide. When divorced from his real Self, however, quite another way unfolds. What unfolds is the way that can never satisfy, because the approach comes out of the false belief that some other consciousness exists and it, rather than his own Truth, can satisfy him.

When living from ego consciousness, my friend Richard is bound to feel separated. The pain of separation sends him seeking the comfort of another in order to feel complete and whole. When feeling separated or divorced from the Truth of our Being, fear and guilt creep in. When lodged in ego consciousness we naturally feel the need to punish ourselves out of guilt. Is it any wonder, then, that we could feel ill at ease with everyday life? When ill at ease, we seek company. Misery likes company, it is said, and now we gnow why this is so. The good news, however, is that we need not stay in the throes of such misery. All it takes is a sudden awareness that there must be a better way, and then to take the first step onto that path.

It takes courage to see beyond the personal and mental, but it takes only obedience or surrender, and not courage anymore, to exercise the Truth found in Wisdom. Through the spiritual we come to gnow that we need not ask for, but rather are, what we seek elsewhere. We simply declare abundance, peace, joy, and harmony as our reality. These are the real spiritual fruits, and they are ours, as inheritors of the Kingdom. And it is to these that we really are wed; as a whole they form an amalgam of Truth. By staying faithful to the spiritual Way, both the personal and mental simply fall away. We do not have to work through them, step by step, after all. Indeed, once aware of our Truth, we see the illusions we have believed as just that, and we move on, freed from all that has held the curtain of untruth in place.

Many still deal with Life mostly on a personal basis. Jesus took many to mental, and some on to spiritual means, those few who found the real spiritual meaning in what he taught. Such persons grew not only to change perspectives about Life, but in discerning the Truth they came to meet and live regularly with the Paraclete, the guide Jesus told us existed, and which would serve us in his absence. Actually, that was his teaching all along, whether he was present or not. Always, always, he told his followers to go inward for the Truth that was theirs. It is only when we live our Truth that the peace and joy we are thrives.

Surrendering as humility

This going within for one's Truth is the ultimate in humility, for it is surrender: surrender of self, with a personal "s," to the Self, with the impersonal divine, "S". Either we can trust divine consciousness for our highest good or we can trust our own view. How good have the personal and mental worked for you, lately? Just how vain are we to even think we are separate from Truth; so much so, that we, in all arrogance, can do better than divine consciousness, or the Christ, that is our very essence of Being?

A brief story could well focus your attention on which holds highest value for you. Again from an unidentified source on Internet, it is a story about two wolves, and it goes like this:

"One evening an old Cherokee told his grandson about a battle that goes on inside people. He said, "My son, the battle is between two 'wolves' inside us all.

One is Evil. It is anger, envy, jealousy, sorrow, regret, greed, arrogance, self-pity, guilt, resentment, inferiority, lies, false pride, superiority, and ego.

The other is Good. It is joy, peace, love, hope, serenity, humility, kindness, benevolence, empathy, generosity, truth, compassion and faith."

The grandson thought about it for a minute and then asked his grandfather: "Which wolf wins?"

The old Cherokee simply replied, "The one you feed".

Indeed, what you feed grows. In a similar way, "what you pay attention to grows." This is the key message of the book and video, *The Secret*; only that's largely about material exercise. What we are dealing with here is the spiritual basis, and only that, for spiritually there is no Truth other than this Truth. Metaphysically speaking, then, there aren't two wolves to feed — for there is nothing but Truth, nothing but divine consciousness, nothing but Wisdom, God, the Christ — and therefore nothing opposed to divine consciousness that we might feed. We only believe that there is and that we must.

Did Jesus not tell us to "Love God with all your heart, mind, soul, and strength and you shall inherit the Kingdom?" Yes, Loving your highest Self, the Truth individualized as Wisdom, with all your heart, mind, soul and strength sets free your

Truth—and all the rest will follow. Notice that no mention is ever made by Jesus, the divine metaphysician, of any material idea. He surely did not tell us to love physicality or that physicality could provide us with all we really want and need—or that belief in anything akin to ego or mass consciousness would do us any good. To the contrary, his teachings stress the importance of paying no attention to anything but the spiritual Truth, and all the rest—good, meaning the fruits of Wisdom—will follow. The spiritual path constitutes the gifts of the Kingdom, the divine or inspirational ideas and conscious awareness that manifest into the material world when we invest in or worship only the Truth.

Such commitment reminds me of a recent conversation I had with a wise friend, Tom, during a walk in the early morning hours. We had not visited with one another in quite a while, seeing that his permanent home is elsewhere, so we stopped to catch up on goings-on with one another. During the spirited conversation he said that he had been supporting me from afar with the writing that was coming through me. He asked what my process was, and after hearing my description, he said this: "That reminds me of what Mark Twain, I think it was, said. He said, if I may paraphrase, 'writing, for him, was like pulling a rope out from space with notes attached to it, not knowing what was going to come next.'" In just that simple sentence, he had described precisely what my process is.

Then he added the ultimate metaphysical question, which pleased me to no end: "The real question," he said, "is, what is it that continually feeds or provides the rope and notes?" Gnowing Tom as I do, especially seeing the glint in his eye as he announced the question, I gnew that the Truth of the matter was already clear to him, just as it was to me. Grace expressed in a single moment became the Truth for all time. In that single moment we were affirmed as One yet again.

The deeper Truth found in this story is for us to acknowledge and activate that which lies in waiting for our awareness to embrace. Divine essence is present in the infinite array of gifts contained in the Truth that resides in us all. Once we become aware of the specific gift in its divine form, it is activated in our Being and, when held in the loving spaciousness surrender commands of us, it grows into the divine effect that is contained in its very fiber. With the divine Truth and its activation being inseparable, what else could manifest but the Loving Way? When we fail to listen to the still, small voice, we instead put into force some form of ego consciousness that can only serve ego. Ego has not as its purpose, nor is it in ego's domain, to serve spiritual ends. Instead, when we move out in our daily practice from the realm of ego consciousness, we are using the immense energy available to us for egocentric purpose. Is that bad? No, it only is what it is, and is not to be judged, only discerned. Actually, it is not what it appears to be, at all. It is only illusion thought to be Truth.

The key is to discern Truth. Is Truth governed by spiritual consciousness, or a belief in ego consciousness? Once discerned, you will gnow without fail that spiritual consciousness is what you really want. If you go to outside authority to see Life through the lenses of the egocentric, material world, this is what will show up for you. But do not be surprised by that any more. Remember, we cannot have it both ways; we cannot serve God, Wisdom, and mammon, the material demands of ego consciousness. Just remember that the latter really does not exist in the spiritual world.

Should you choose the latter, ego consciousness, and later come to regret it, fear not. All it takes to reverse the pattern is an awakening to the awareness of the Truth, and practicing the exercise of this awareness until it returns you to the perfection of Being you already are and have simply forgotten. It is said that what we choose, we remember; what we don't choose, we forget. Remember that Life is not about choice; it is about gnowing the Truth and surrendering to it. While in ego consciousness, we think we choose wisely. Just gnow that ego will fight you for this the entire way, out of its fear of being replaced. You can avoid the fight by exercising the awareness that there is only One way, thus eradicating choice as an option altogether—and duality along with it.

The idea of rendering what is given us to render is reinforced in a piece by William Roedel Rathvon, found in Vol. I of his Association Addresses, (1912-1938). He adds this fuel to the fire of enthusiasm for the Truth heard.

"Fresh opportunities are constantly arising. We must remember that while opportunity is always provided, we often have to hunt for it; so don't wait for it, but go after it. It can be made out of ordinary circumstances or conditions. But when it is insight, promptness is needed. Do not wait for it to come around again, for it may forget where you live. It is a case of striking while the iron is hot. If the iron is not hot, you can make it so by striking the same place until it gets hot. If opportunity sometimes hides, perseverance finds it; if it flees, chase it; and 'despise not the day of small things,' for little opportunities often grow into big actualities." (p. 6)

"Amen," I say to that!

Forgetfulness

Some forget their foundation of Wisdom and behave irresponsibly, erratically. No matter what, we give Love and respect automatically to the spiritual Being because it is divine essence and thus good. This is how we can come to love Hitler, and Saddam Hussein, and even the rapist. Out of this gnowing, we thus comprehend that as soon as we call one evil, all must also be evil. Just so, each is good, and once we render someone good, all must be that. It is interesting to watch who we exclude, and why, from either list.

This does not mean that we should not hold people responsible for their offenses. Those acts that form out of ego consciousness—what we see as evil—form because of belief in a life separate from God. Despite the abiding Love we give unabashedly to the essence of the "offender," however, the one who has expressed the offense out of his ego conscious nature must earn respect from, and receive justice in, the world of his choosing.

As a case in point, recently I was talking with a friend who described to me the gist of a conversation she had with her husband in the confines of their counselor. The husband was demanding respect from his family because he was the father and thus deserved it, simply because he was the father. Where he got that idea no one can say, I suspect. Nevertheless, the counselor responded: "I can see you believe that. Let me tell you that I have many couples that come in here where one or the other parent is abusing the children. Should those children be expected to respect these parents just because of their biological role even though they are being abused?"

This made it plain enough. Each of us must hold ourselves accountable for what we demonstrate, no matter how we label it, and despite the real Truth of our Being. As long as we choose ego consciousness as the realm from which to render meaning, that is the price we must pay. If we are to dance in this realm, we must indeed pay the fiddler.

At the seat of ego consciousness we paint with the illusions of untruth, and these images fill the canvas our Life becomes. On the other hand, when we reside in Wisdom, the real treasure is activated into Being. All the rest comes into that same awareness, and our canvas resonates with Soul.

If our creation begins with a view of Life as divine essence, divine essence it will Be. If not, well, we can get many material things worked out, and material benefits derived, but do those really last, and do they serve any real purpose? Do any of these give us real peace of mind, fill our heart with joy, or help gain enthusiasm for our journey? What is it we wish to exercise throughout eternity: material collections or the fruits of Wisdom?

Prosperity, the essence of our Being, is a function of spiritual demonstration, not material accumulation. Spiritual prosperity is about peace of mind, a joyful heart, an attitude of gratitude, and the abundance of divine ideas with which to guide our lives. At the heart of our description of prosperity must be the gift of Wisdom that sets it free. So, all we need do is invest our conviction in this definition of abundance and we shall inherit the Kingdom. Indeed, we then are being what we want to see.

Only the best

So many ask: "How do I know what is best for me, the Truth of what I am, for me?" We've already spoken about the still, small voice that speaks from the silence of our Being. The simplest answer, then, is this: just listen in your heart of hearts for the Truth. What does that look like? Here's one example.

Some time ago I was visiting one of my family on the West Coast. While there I had lunch with a long-time friend. He was recovering from a recent divorce and needed a friendly ear. Having just sold his house and feeling quite alone, he began telling me that he had no idea what to do with the rest of his life. First, we ran through all his current options, for which he had no enthusiasm at all. As he listed them, one by one by one, his tone was flat, his interest low, and he dismissed them out of hand. Was there any of them he could not do? Of course not; he could do all of them, and well. But he wisely did not want to do something just for the sake of doing it.

Eventually, as he got to the end of his list, all of a sudden he became alive. He had always wanted to travel, and excitedly began to list places he wanted to go and people he had wanted to visit for years. To say he lit up like a Christmas tree at the Rockefeller Center is no exaggeration. "Are you listening to yourself?" I asked.

"No, what do you mean?" he responded.

"Well," I began, "with all the other things you offered up as possibilities, you were flat, no enthusiasm whatsoever. Now, with this, you are alive with energy; you are smiling, really enjoying the idea."

"So," he said, "so what?"

"So what? Here's what," I responded. "Enthusiasm, passion for Life, is what it means to be with your highest Self, with God. It is the clearest signal that this is the Truth for you."

"Really?" he rejoined, "but I have a responsibility, I can't go anywhere."

"A responsibility to what or to whom?" I asked, curiously. "To the money I made on the sale of my house."

"A responsibility to your money?" I challenged him. "What about the responsibility to fulfill your soul's longing? When will you honor that?"

"Oh, gosh!" he exclaimed. "You just gave me permission to do this."

"No," I responded in earnest, "you just gave yourself permission to consider the Truth for you."

We then worked over his finances, and in no time at all we tallied the rent for the apartment he was about to move into, the anticipated cost of utilities, the benefit of no car payment or gasoline cost, no cable TV, and all the money he would have spent on food, moving, and the like. He even volunteered that he'd have no trouble selling his furniture instead of storing it while he traveled. He was ecstatic. I had never before seen him like this and told him so. When we parted, he was going to complete his plans to feed his enthusiasm.

A few days later, he E-mailed me to say that things were moving right along and that I would be surprised at how far he had gotten in his planning. Then, in another day or two, he called to say that he just couldn't do it. He had done "due diligence," and all this was more complicated than he had originally thought. "Oh, no," I remember thinking, "the ego has gotten a hold on him." "Besides," he said, "I just don't want to do this alone." "What became of nourishing your soul, and the enthusiasm you had for the Truth you heard?" I asked. "Well," he responded, "that will just have to wait." I could have cried for him, but it is his Life, and I have no right to live it for him. Only he can do that. As my wise father used to say: "If I put my head on your shoulders, you would not be you." This is a good adage to apply in such situations.

I tell you this story for two reasons. The first is that the voice of enthusiasm and passion for expressing the Truth are of primary importance. These are what make us alive and what ignites the soul—and what should be followed if we are to honor our spiritual Being. Just be sure you do not confuse the more superficial level of excitement, much like infatuation, with genuine enthusiasm and passion, and you will always be in touch with what is really best for you.

Second, I tell you this because of the obvious culprit that kept my friend from exercising this inalienable right: the abject fear of being alone, for it keeps us in relationships and jobs that no longer serve us, and places us in situation after situation that are absolutely wrong for us. If only he could have seen that following one's enthusiasm eliminates such fear. All it takes is the first step, and fear disappears.

As I heard from the still, small voice during a special prayer method years ago: "You want all the answers before you begin. All you have to do is start, and I will reveal what you need to know as you go along. The first step is all you need take right now." This is another way of saying, "Love God (your Truth, Wisdom) with all your heart, mind, soul and strength and all the rest will be given unto you." This divine presence and commitment is what keeps us from being alone. And what guides us as we enthusiastically express Wisdom in each present moment. All we need do is take that glorious first step, rather than staying mired in fear.

Another sad thing about my friend's decision is that by not nourishing his soul he had placed himself exactly where he did not want to be, under the rule of his ego consciousness yet again: all alone in his new apartment, stewing over having not made another choice. He was not a happy camper. If only he could have seen that none of us is ever really alone. How could we be alone when we are all really One? It is our current state of consciousness that holds us in a particular frame of mind, after all.

Unfortunately, when we adhere to the ego's ways we end up feeling alone, separate, and governed by fear. That is the ego's lair; it is the trap or web that imprisons us, the government that habitually does us in. When we acknowledge the conscious awareness of the voice of Wisdom, then all these limitations disappear from view, and we receive—yes, you guessed it—all the gifts of the Kingdom.

One of the beliefs haunting us in such deliberations is the false parallel drawn between being alone and being lonely. If I have become aware of the happiness, peace and joy I really am, just where is the room for loneliness? No matter what, when I'm in touch with my spiritual reality, it matters not whether I am alone or in the company of others. I am still what I Am, and no one can change that, one way or another. And at no time have I heard what I am called "alone."

Many think it is Life that builds character. Spiritually speaking, Life's challenges do not build character at all. They reveal it. Either you have what it takes, or you do not. Actually, we all have it as we become aware of its depth and breadth. And we act from it, or the lack of it. Either way, it works. What it takes is going within to hear the True character of Being and then allowing that to flourish without fail. This is real character, which comes out of the power of awareness.

Character is not something we build because some external

force raises the bar of expectation. Real character comes out of genuine humility. Indeed, real character is about being humble enough to get out of one's own way, in favor of listening in order to hear the Truth rendered in the voice of Wisdom. Being, acting in our Truth, is what gives us the power of Spirit. This is humility defined. Without humility we are only following our belief in the ego's beckoning, from and within which character cannot be found. Really, we all have character. We just need to become aware of our *real* character—and then simply demonstrate it under all circumstances and conditions.

Creation: the bottom line

Creation is a funny thing. As I posited in another book, "What If...?," creation seems to speak in a variety of ways. Sometimes it speaks out of ego consciousness, while at others, from the divinity we are:

"We create constantly, yet fail to acknowledge Creation as our natural way of Life. Whether one connects with the idea of a divine Creator or not, surely one can come to the understanding that most everything we do and say is an act of Creation. We create words and phrases and sentences galore. We create looks of all kinds, gestures without end. We create art and stories and friendships, even enemies. We create war and not much peace, animosity and not much forgiveness. We create scrumptious meals, renewal through spring-cleaning, renovation of homes, old and not so old. We create inspiration, often times unwittingly, yet always profoundly. We create welcome and warmth of Being, receptivity, and spiritual awareness. We create more room for enlightenment and insight. We create and create and create.

This is our most natural expression: Creation. Yet we rarely attribute what we'd call our creations to the example set by the

Creation of what we are. Each Crea-tion stems from an idea, even if only briefly acknowledged or known. And each, when embraced by conviction or faith, comes to fruition, though not always pre-cisely as envisioned. The point is that each does come to fruition, bears the fruit of the one from whom the seed comes. When we get out of our own way and let the Idea flow from the seat of our divinity, that, too, bears Fruit, but of a different kind. Yet both kinds of fruit, that of egoism and of divinity, are in the perfect im-age and likeness of intention or the founding idea/Idea.

Our function is what we call Creation: to remember only that we are divine Beings, and from our Essence—our most natural function—our divine purpose is to produce divine fruit. In either case, the fruit is perfect, that is, perfectly formed from its founder, and thus not to be judged but rather discerned. When we see the fruit we can easily discern from which seed it comes and can adjust Creation to fit the Truth of what we are: Creation individualized and individuated. And yet in Creation we are at and as One." (p. 18)

Strangely, we also seem to create out of ideas that are not divine; those that stem from our belief in ego consciousness, as well as those we have taken as true from collective or mass consciousness. We demonstrate misery, failure, tension, wars, difference, and deceit. Even some seemingly "good" creations come to the fore out of ego consciousness. Similarly, each of these has its forbearers in the holding place of ego consciousness. Truth is, only those creations that stem from inner Truth reflect Truth. While others may seem to do so, they are merely reflec-tions of ego misunderstood. Just because we do what might please someone does not mean it is the reflection of the highest good to be demonstrated in the moment. Do not let the appearance of good lull you to sleep, when living from Wisdom brings enthusiasm for Life to the fore.

The central point to remember is that when we see the effects of our belief in ego consciousness—and they are clearly represented in our daily existence—let this be a clue, and cue, to return to divine consciousness as the only real cause of Creation. As in all of spiritual Life, to begin in and as the Truth not only establishes Truth as the only real Being, it also guarantees a Life of nothing but Truth expressed in our individualization of the way. It is for this that we are here. This is our purpose and description of Being at One. This is the way, the Truth and Life of which Jesus spoke and taught.

Daring to Differ

I'd like to risk a shift in perspective at this point, and say that Life is about demonstrating inspiration heard inwardly, and not about creating at all. There is a big difference between the idea of creating and spiritual demonstration. Life is not about magic, something we have labeled creation—turning nothing into something. Life is about validating the evidence of Truth, Christ consciousness, inspiration made aware—bringing the face of that evidence out into the open as we witness its Source. What we thus are demonstrating is that we are being at One with Truth.

Our purpose deals with the act of being fulfilled by demonstrating the voice of inspirational vibration, the resonance with Truth heard inwardly. From a metaphysical point of view, the single criterion for validating spiritual demonstration is to discern if what we are demonstrating is coming from the one real Source. Period! We either began our demonstration at the Source or we did not; either we demonstrate spiritual Source or we are demonstrating no thing at all. This may seem too far for us to stretch just yet, but I ask you to consider the suggested shift and see where it takes you. Just revisit the previous paragraphs dealing with creation and substitute the term demonstration for creation and see if any meaningful shift occurs to you. That said, until and unless you can see some real difference between creation and demonstration, by all means stick with creation.

Biblical creation

Are you prepared for a treatment of spiritual Biblical meaning? In many religious circles, we mostly take the Bible as the literal Word we are to follow. Metaphysically, this is as far from Truth as it can be. As cited earlier, Jesus said we are to view Life and God spiritually, as symbolic form of real meaning. With this as our context let us understand that there are essentially only two sections of the Bible that describe spiritual Life. All the rest is a depiction—one allegory after another, as it were—that describes the ego's god. The ego's god is a god of separation, vengeance, and who keeps track of all we think and do, so he can exercise final judgment on us. It also speaks of a god we can manipulate with our behavior, as though we have the power to somehow make such a god respond more favorably to us—or, to the contrary, that we can make this god angry by behaving badly. This illusory view is what has most of us working hard at being "good enough," so we can avoid God's punishment. It also has us placing blame outside ourselves, so we can be rendered guilt free—and working beyond our calling just to earn favor from a fictitious god.

In the first chapter of Genesis we find the allegory depicting Creation as the Truth of divine idea expressed: only divine consciousness or God creates spiritual reality. Allegories as a whole tell Truth through story, using symbolic characters. Forget the details and descriptions; they don't really account for much. Rather, listen for what symbolism tells us. The only thing that counts is the resonance we hear within when we read or hear these stories. So, in this first chapter we see that it is God (spiritual consciousness) that demonstrates.

The second and third chapters of Genesis go on to describe what happens when we are asleep to the Truth, told through the story of Adam and Eve. From a superficial and spiritually naive mediation of this allegory, we easily could come to think it is we who are to create. Asleep as Adam was, he came to believe the dream that had Eve created out of his rib, or matter. The allegory goes further, declaring we want something we think God has, but are all too easily influenced by outside authority and think something better can be found elsewhere. So we "go it alone," only to find ourselves standing naked before God, living an erroneous or dream-like existence. This dream world is not at all real, but we have come to think it is. And we use the illusion to hold ourselves in our state of separation. We gnow this depiction comes from ego consciousness because of the reference to shame and guilt. These are not found inward. All that follows in this dream are signs of the fear we live in. Because on some level we have come to believe this story is the Truth, our perpetually felt fear is that God will one day avenge us for our dastardly sin of separating ourselves from the "One and only."

We can see the parallel of this story with the way we live our lives in ego consciousness if we would just think of our experience in this body as walking in our sleep. If you have ever seen someone sleepwalking, you undoubtedly have come to understand that even though the person sleepwalking most often has his eyes closed, he travels throughout his dream or nightmare without harm. It is as though his eyes were open. The lives we experience in this physical body are essentially just like sleep-walking, for if we learn to look at what is happening as we sleepwalk in symbolic terms, we will soon come to see the real value of this existence. As an outer experience it is illusion seeming real. In this way, it is just like the allegory of Adam and Eve, with all the unfounded imagery seeming to be real when it is not that at all. We make it up as we go, often using false information we have taken in from mass or collective consciousness as our foundation of belief. Just as in a sleeping dream, we can watch and change its outcome, yet it is still nothing but symbolism or deeper meaning waiting to be discovered. Allegory shows its own face of reality, treating us to the single meaning and purpose of its existence, the details and appearances notwithstanding.

Even though we find what appears to be some lovely language and stories in the Bible, they all relate to a God separate from us. This shows that although the dream is an illusion, illusion can seem rather pleasant at times. This is the illusion ego wants us to believe. Of course, "pleasant" is a relative term. Relativity, comparison and contrast are found only in ego consciousness. Truth is the absolute principle, and there is no relativity, comparison or contrast to be found there.

It is not until we get to the allegories containing the teachings of Jesus that the other examples of Truth are brought to light. Even here, we see the difference in view between Jesus and the Pharisees being revealed on the stage of comparison and contrast. This is the clue that such difference is a depiction of ego consciousness on the part of the Pharisees. However, when we bring Jesus' teachings to metaphorical or symbolic meaning, we see that they all refer to the Truth that can be found only in silence. Once the spiritual meaning of the Principle Jesus applies to Life comes into full awareness, the ego consciousness renderings represented by the Pharisaic view are seen for the illusions they are. They disappear from view in our remembrance of Truth. And we walk in Truth only from then on. This was Jesus' admonition to us, regularly expressed in his words and ways.

This Truth or Wisdom we now demonstrate is finally revealed as the "hidden secret," the spiritual Truth that has been hidden by our temporary commitment to illusion, the false dream. The "hidden secret" is this: all the while, there has been a single Truth faithfully abiding our spirituality. The One and only Truth is that we are conscious awareness individualized, and not separate from that. It is this single Truth that we call the Holy Spirit. Jesus called it a guide or the Paraclete. I call it Wisdom. It is the infinitely voiced single Truth that keeps calling us to be expressed, no matter how far we stray from it—no matter how separate we feel from it. Faithful to the end, we are drawn back to full awareness of Being.

Because of various dogmatic religious teachings, this description of the Bible's purpose sounds unusual, crazy even. Given a spiritual context, we come to see that Wisdom speaks to erase the insanity of duality. Life is spiritual, and not the illusory appearance we abide in ego consciousness. In this way, Science and Health, The Infinite Way, The Science of Mind, and A Course in Miracles are fair companions to the Bible. Each speaks to the Truth while also dramatically pointing to the way of ego consciousness. All of these methods depict Life in rather exaggerated form. Subtlety is not easily discerned from the seat of ego consciousness. The veil of illusion hides Truth from view.

Demonstration as Truth spoken

Once we are spiritually aware, we comprehend that Scripture can lead us to Truth, despite its primary reference to illusion. Here's one example of what we can draw from illusion using spiritual discernment. In the Apocalypse, John reported: "And I saw a new heaven and a new earth: for the first heaven and the first earth were passed away; and there was no more sea." When taken literally, this makes little sense at all. It could easily sound like a hallucination. When taken symbolically, the sea depicts the often turbulent and stormy illusions of ego consciousness that ebb and flow—but no more are. The new heaven and earth speak to the Wisdom that flows from inspirational idea to earthly demonstration. The illusion of duality, the purported co-existence of ego with God, lives no more. Only Truth remains. Spiritual consciousness demonstrates only what it is.

Let us take another look at Scripture, even if only to sharpen our translational eye. What follows are two sets of Scriptural references, the first from I Thessalonians 5:5-8. The second is from Ephesians 4: 17, 18, 20-24. Individually and in the collective they define awareness of inner Truth as the catalyst for demonstrating that Truth. From I Thessalonians, then, we see these words. Each phrase or sentence is followed by its spiritual translation. Listen for inner resonance. Form your own translation of Truth this way.

"Ye are all the children of light, and the children of the day: we are not of the night, or of darkness."

Each inspirational idea is parented by its divine origin, and individually demonstrated. As a virginal idea individualized, each is only from inspiration and for enlightenment, not ignorance or darkness.

"Therefore, let us not sleep, as do others; but let us watch and be sober."

Therefore, let us be ever alert and aware, letting awareness of Wisdom be what we take seriously.

"For they that sleep are asleep in the night; and they that be drunken are drunken in the night."

For those that fall asleep to the Truth, life is illusion based on ignorance; and they that drink of illusion live in that same ignorance, in darkness.

"But let us, who are of the day, be sober, putting on the breastplate of faith and love; and for an helmet, the hope of salvation."

Let us who live from inner enlightenment understand that it

is this that calls our devotion, and is what we are, Love; spiritual enlightenment demonstrated is our ultimate protection, our sure salvation from need of hope.

And from Ephesians:

"This I say therefore, and testify in the Lord, that ye henceforth walk not as the Gentiles walk, in the vanity of their mind."

When we attest to the Law of Order, we walk not in ego consciousness—not enveloped in the vanity that attributes reality to a self that is separate from God.

"Having the understanding darkened, being alienated from the life of God through ignorance that is in them, because of blindness of the heart."

Out of ignorance, spiritual awareness is darkened and alienated from Truth. When we live from the illusion of ego consciousness, we are rendered blind to the Truth found only in the depths of our hearts.

"But ye have not so learned Christ;"

Sitting in the lap of ignorance, we have not seen the way to enlightenment, but we who are aware and awake have learned that the Christ is the Truth conveyed by the voice of Wisdom heard in silence.

"If so be that ye have heard him, and have been taught by him, as the truth is in Jesus."

As we listen to the Christ or the voice of Wisdom that guides only to our highest good, we comprehend that this is the One true Way, just as Jesus saw this as the Way for him.

"That ye put off concerning the former conversation the old man, which is corrupt according to the deceitful lusts."

Following Christ consciousness puts off our investment and faith in ego consciousness. As a potential pathway to Truth, ego consciousness is corrupt and deceitful in the ways it leads us only to lusts, our infatuations or dreams, instead of expressing our inner Truth.

"And be renewed in the spirit of your mind;"

This renewal is of spiritual guidance, found in the gifts of divine Mind, which is eternally and infinitely expressed divine consciousness, Wisdom.

"And that ye put on the new man, which after God is created in righteousness and true holiness."

In this renewal we put on a new idea of our existence, which is to live only from divine consciousness. Truly, this is the only righteous demonstration, the only true holiness, the One.

There is no duality in the spiritual translation of this Scripture. Only the One speaks our renewed comprehension of spiritual Life. This defines our purpose, and thus can be our only manifestation or demonstration. This section ends with a spiritual translation of what has been called the Lord's Prayer. While about prayer, this translation is more about loving Life and our place in it enough to take lead from the only source of Truth for us.

When asked how it is we are to pray, Jesus answered with

suggested language. We should place Jesus' response in the context of his faithful admonition that we should pray by going within, and in secret, not publicly. Within, as we gnow by now, is not a physical location. Within is the symbolic location of the Christ that speaks in silence. And we should shut out any outside reference, silence it—any and all ideas, desires, requests for change, beliefs, and opinions. These represent what ego consciousness would want us to accept as real and the Truth. Actually, when acting as disciples of the belief in ego consciousness, the illusions or myths we've established are taken on as a way of avoiding Truth.

When pushed further, it is almost out of exasperation that Jesus seems to be saying, "Well, if you insist on praying aloud, at least understand what Life is about. Life is about demonstrating spiritual awareness, for the conscious awareness of inner Wisdom is what parents the Wisdom into Being." It is by seeing Life in this spiritual context that we finally understand the single divine principle we are to follow. Demonstrating Life faithful to this principle, we express the only true form of love from day to day, moment by moment. Finally, we live and experience our purpose and meaning authentically.

The term "Lord" as used below is an abbreviation for The Law of Order. This spiritual law says that when aware, we hear only highest good spoken, and the awareness is what activates it into Being. This is the gnowing of the Truth that makes us free to express it thus. Metaphorically, "as in Heaven, so in earth." Such discernment renders duality obsolete, falling away from its own weight of illusion.

The Lord's Prayer	The Law of Order
"Our Father which art in heaven	That which parents spiritual demonstration emanates from conscious awareness

hallowed be thy name;	and holds only sacred meaning;
thy kingdom come,	conscious awareness of Wisdom fulfills purpose,
thy will be done	with Truth begetting only Truth,
on earth as it is in heaven;	demonstrated precisely as its Source;
give us this day our daily bread,	awareness reveals the infinite supply of Wisdom,
and forgive us our debts	releasing erroneous beliefs and opinions
as we forgive our debtors;	and the false teachings of the collective consciousness;
lead us not into temptation	we claim only inner Truth
and deliver us from evil,	and shut the door to duality;
for thine is the kingdom,	spiritual consciousness is the only reality,
the power,	the One and only power,
and the glory, forever.	bringing glory to the infinitude and immortality of authentic demonstration.

Amen.   And so It is.

Seen as one continuous form of outer prayer expressing inner, spiritual meaning, the Lord's Prayer (the prayer of Law of Order), looks like this. It is not to be prayed at all. It is but a statement of inner Truth needing only to be activated out of conscious awareness. Taken to heart, so to speak, the authentic expression of Wisdom thus becomes both our purpose and identity.

That which parents spiritual demonstration emanates from conscious awareness and holds only sacred meaning. Conscious awareness of Wisdom fulfills purpose, with Truth begetting only Truth, demonstrated precisely as its Source. Awareness reveals the infinite supply of Wisdom, releasing erroneous beliefs and opinions and the false teachings of the collective consciousness. We claim only inner Truth and shut the door to duality. Spiritual consciousness is the only reality, the One and only power, bringing glory to the infinitude and immortality of authentic demonstration. And so It is.

And so you Be. Indeed, divine demonstration is the result of Truth activated.

Chapter Six

Principle 4: Expressing the faith *of* God is the key to spiritual fulfillment

"It is wise to listen,....
not to me but to the Word,
and to confess that all things are one...."
Heraclitus

God Itself

We must be careful to discern the distinction between expressing our faith *in* God and expressing the faith *of* God. We'll begin this way. The fulfillment we speak of in this principle is related to conscious awareness of Wisdom and what it produces. We are the perfection of this consciousness individualized. When we say we're placing our faith *in* God, unless we're advanced enough to understand that God is really nothing but our Highest Self, we will have separated ourselves *from* God, the Truth of our Being. In the process, we will have set ourselves up for the pain and suffering that separation engenders. It cannot fail. Separation from the Truth works just that way.

By separating ourselves from the Truth, we also make God into some kind of Santa Claus, an external gift-giver to whom we pray or beg for goods and services. In this context, we also end up saying things like, "How could God have let this child die, or that war happen?" Or, "Why did God heal this person and not that one?" God knows nothing of such things. Wisdom has no such vocabulary. Its only vocabulary is that of Truth, and Truth is only sacred and spiritual, not worldly or material in nature, and disease, war, and death are not found there.How many have prayed for such to end or change, only to find that such requests are not dealt with? Wars go on, people die, and yet we thank God that more have not died in vain. Because such prayers do not seem to be answered, does this mean that there is no real God, or that we are not good enough to have our prayers honored? Or that God does not know of such things and thus cannot trouble itself with them? Does it say that we have placed our conviction in the lap of some external idol to worship, one of the many false gods to which we pray—instead of understanding the real God of the spiritual world, that functions only on a spiritual level? These beliefs are the result of mankind's wounded view that humans are separate from the Wisdom they impart when consciously aware.

Some ideas about faith

Some take faith to mean the trust they put in the church to which they belong, or the religion to which they subscribe. One is asked, "What is your faith?" and the answer sounds something like this: "Oh, I'm a Christian," "I'm a Methodist," or "I'm Muslim."

Some put their faith in God, in church, or even their spouse. In religious doctrine, faith refers to some outer authority in which we place our trust. In such a reference to faith we immediately have created a dualistic life and one of separation from the very God we say we have faith in.

Still another way to deal with the meaning of faith is to see it in a metaphysical context. Metaphysical faith refers to the duty or commitment to fulfill only what we are, divine idea or Wisdom individualized. In this understanding we often say we are keeping faith. Just what is it we are honoring by duty or commitment? We are honoring the Truth we find as we listen in the stillness of our hearts, the meaning and direction we gain from our Highest Self. In this way, the faith we express is honoring the inseparability of Wisdom and its demonstration. The fulfillment of the demonstration is contained in Wisdom itself, just as whatever the oak tree needs for fulfillment is contained in the acorn from which it rises. In both cases, the sacred effect or seeming miracle arrives out of the commitment of that which nourishes it. In the case of the oak tree, nourishment is about soil and sunshine and water. In the case of humans, demonstration is about the nourishment found in our awareness, activated by the Truth heard inwardly.

The faith of God is exhibited by fulfilling a commitment only to a single gift of Truth discerned from its endless source of Wisdom. The inspirational gift is fulfilled simply through our awareness of the idea, which finds activation from the natural expression of our Being. All we need to remember is that God and we are One.

It is this inseparability that defines the faith *of* God. The faith *of* God becomes our spiritual reality as long as we activate Life out of that framework. That to which we give faith will be fulfilled in its likeness.

Having said that, there is one legitimate context for having faith in God. The only way the faith *of* God can be an activation of Truth is when we understand God's real nature—and thus *our* real nature. As we gnow by now, God's perfection is exercised through the activation of Wisdom, the Christ we call spiritual awareness. Therefore, because of God's perfection of Being, to say that we have faith *in* God is to say that we are expressing faith in our perfection of Being. Metaphysically speaking, then, faith is fulfillment befitting what we are, moment-by- moment, gnowing that the effects of such fulfillment is nothing but a reflection of that perfection of Being. Such is the inseparability of Oneness.

In reality, this demonstration is the only real justice that can be levied onto Life. To do otherwise—to live from a basis of, or a false belief in, ego or mass consciousness—is unjust. It's unjust because it shifts the Truth of Being into error, the only real unjust effect perpetrated onto humankind. Said another way, demon-stration of Truth is the only real form of integrity; all else clearly demonstrates the lack thereof.

To simplify even further, to live in our spiritual integrity is the only real justice we can apply to Life. Otherwise, Life becomes unjust and reflects that injustice everywhere. How can giving Life something less than or other than our Truth of Being be just to the world? When we think about wanting justice to be served in a particular situation or circumstance, we might well want to apply this metaphysical standard to Life. Otherwise, real justice will not have been served. Instead some cold, judgmental application would have been applied, and from this only a few steps towards real justice can be the result. Why not apply the metaphysical standard to all that Life brings us, so real justice can reign throughout? It is in this awareness that justice is truly served.

The is and isn't of prayer

This kind of faith, the faith *of* God, renders prayer unnecessary, at least as most of us practice prayer: as a plea for mercy or healing or change. We may feel good when we do it, yet the fact that those who are so-called praying are engaging their religious commitment in the moment for another's good speaks to the power of their sacred intention and not to the power of prayer itself. Metaphysically, prayer is unnecessary because all is already complete and perfect. So what is to pray for—to be happy, fulfilled, prosperous, healed and secure? Such things already exist at the heart of our sacred consciousness.

In another sense, inviting God into our physical experience is tantamount to inviting God into ego consciousness. How unjust can that be? How can perfection hold our self-created dream as real? Wisdom gnows nothing of ego consciousness, because ego consciousness is only a dream. Thus we gain the direction to shut our mouths and listen only to Wisdom, being obedient and surrendering to Life's calling for us.

It is only we who apply our limited thinking to manifest some relatively minor effect in Wisdom's place, like a larger house, yet another car or a special companion. Such desires make a mockery of real prayer. To pray that way is to make God in our image, an ill-formed image of ego consciousness. Thus we imbed the false notion of duality yet again. Only in Wisdom or God is prayer found, and already answered. All prayer needs is our conscious awareness in order to activate it into Being.

On the opposite side of the fence from Wisdom, the only real consciousness, we, in our conviction of a world apart, produce war and poverty. We create war and poverty in the world of separation, the material world of duality. Thus it is ours to fix, not for some entity separate from us we call God. To invite God into ego consciousness is to invite Wisdom into nothingness. How can "no thing" benefit anyone or anything?

We only need to remember to stay in our awareness of Wisdom's perfection, and war and poverty disappear in that consciousness. While expressing our Being as Wisdom we can hardly be confused by the erroneous ideas of war and poverty, despite their appearance. Yet, in the state of ego consciousness, there are many who do exactly that: confuse the two, even to the point that they self-righteously think they are being spiritually correct when activating war and acts that contribute to poverty of any kind, in any place.

So, why should we pray for something we already are or have? It's all about what consciousness we're allied with. Joel Goldsmith, father of the powerful Infinite Way work, tells us that it is paganistic to pray for God to remove what does not exist. And it is heathenish to pray to God to do God's own work in caring for the universe. Our task, then, is to look beyond such illusions to find the Truth that Wisdom is eternal, infinite, and immortal. Like begets like, after all.

We do not pray for good in our head or with our mouths, through our words. Prayer is listening for the affirmation of the eternal presence of Wisdom in our heart. Being centered in

Wisdom—the Truth itself—denies the presence of any belief that is counter to Truth. Said in perhaps an even stronger way, prayer, as usually practiced, is the ego's tool and a projection of erroneous need. How can we righteously pray for need when we are already complete? There is no counter force or power or need separate from that embedded in Wisdom. There is only Wisdom, period. All the rest testifies to a belief in separation from Wisdom.

This is the absolute in prayer: communion with inner Truth, Wisdom, the Highest Good. "Go into your closet and pray," Jesus told us, meaning to listen to the voice heard in our heart of hearts, of course. It is there where we find the bread (inner gnowing) and wine (spiritual activation) of which the material plane knows not. It is the Truth and its activation of which we are now aware, and to which we are now to commit all our conviction, our faith—the faith *of* God. Expressing the faith of God is the key to spiritual fulfillment.

Chapter Seven

Principle 5: Service to your inner Truth is the highest form of Love

"If you send forth only the messengers
the Holy Spirit gives you,
wanting no message but theirs,
you will see fear no more."
A Course in Miracles

Love lived

I suspect most people see love as a series of acts that seem to show we care about others. "I love you," we say, and out of that verbal expression we engage with others in acts of kindness and caring: everything from a gentle smile or hug in a time of need to bringing food to a neighbor when in despair, all the way to bringing home a dozen roses or box of candy just to celebrate the the one loved. On it goes, throughout the days and months and years, expressing the feeling that we care for someone besides ourselves. These are good things to do, and are glimpses of the loving way.

Yet, often, these expressions are not real signs of authentic Love in the ultimate sense. As good as these examples are, and many more like them, often they are but an extension of the best side of our ego consciousness. This is largely because we are rarely in touch with Wisdom. We are living under the influence of the collective consciousness and the callousness engendered by the fast-paced egocentric express train many of us are on. Much of the time our actions only reflect our never-ending compulsion to overcome the guilt that festers beneath the skin of ego consciousness. Such expressions are only an illusion dressed up to make us think they are real and the Truth. It is said that the greatest sign of real Love is the giving of one's life for another—but even this, believe it or not—is not the ultimate gift of Love.

The greatest sign of Love is not that we lay down our physical life for another, even as noble as that is. The real demonstration of love is that we lay down the ego's way for the spiritual. This serves our deepest inner calling and brings integrity of Being and fullness of dignity to Life. Thus is authenticity defined. Setting aside ego consciousness for the Truth defines spiritual intimacy—that invisible servant which brings us home, at last, to our authentic Being.

What more Love can we give the world than to be intimate with the Truth of what we are, our most authentic selves? What a remarkable example of Wisdom for all to live and Be! Living true to our inner calling is our only work, our only business. All others have the same business we do. We just need to let them do it, or help them become aware of the need to do it, but only when asked. And then just be there for them instead of trying or feeling the need to change them. Changing others is none of our business. Somewhere I read that God was satisfied simply to create the world; it is only we who feel the need to both create *and* change the world.

Feeling the need to change others or the world comes off as a need to be judgmental. The Truth of the matter is that it is the one who wants the other to change that must come to grips with those very same traits within himself, or his intolerance of them. What is the "cure" for such a perspective? The cure is about taking your Life back. When we focus on desired change in another it's tantamount to giving those pieces within us to another. Some call this "giving our soul away." It is not really that, but projection is close to it, for we expend or project our emotional, psychic, and spiritual energy on an illusion we're really trying to heal in ourselves, onto another. In this sense we are indeed giving away a view of ourselves so we don't have to deal inwardly with it.

Instead, we must repent, go in another direction—the direction that uses these same judgments as a way of redirecting the desired changes to be done within oneself. By doing so, we loosen those erroneous evaluations that seem too painful and too strong to deal with. When we take our Life back, we expose those fearful thoughts about ourselves and find behind them the Truth that we are One, simply awaiting the conscious awareness that will set Truth free. We have just momentarily forgotten the sacred process of spiritual demonstration and need only a gentle reminder to recoup the Truth and express it thus.

This kind of service, living authentically, is the highest form of Life and Love. It is the highest form of service because as we fulfill our highest calling to express only Wisdom, this is what brings the fullness of purpose to Life. When we listen even further, we will come to gnow, without a shadow of a doubt, precisely in what form we are to exercise our Truth. In the larger context of eternity, we get to live or express our inner Truth through *all* we do. That reality is what makes us really alive—and what forms the highest service we can Be to all.

Alive with enthusiasm and passion

I recently reviewed a short photo essay and written commentary by Jan Saudek, the brilliant Czechoslovakian photographer—stunningly beautiful in all regards. It reminded me of the feeling I get when I allow my true Self to be fully immersed in this glorious gift Life is. Saudek says it this way: "I'm here where I belong; I'm alive," where his passion for what he is is best expressed, I might add.

To be able to gnow and act alive in our Life's calling is magical—and the expression of Truth, all wrapped in One. How joyful it is, and how alive we are! I suppose this is the true definition of enthusiasm and passion: to be alive with, and as, what one is called to Be. This investment in loyalty to our real identity fulfills our purpose. Authentic fulfillment can never come from all our "doings" as we play various roles. Fulfillment comes only from expressing what we gnow to be the Truth for us, no matter what.

The so-called bottom line, then, is that while it takes courage to hear the voice of your enthusiasm instead of the ego, it is obedience or surrender to what we're enthusiastic and passionate about that brings our Truth to fruition. Enthusiasm means "in the presence of God; with God; on fire with God; at One with our Highest Self, Wisdom." What could be better? To be other than that is to be at the doorstep and beckoning call of abject fear. I do not know about you, but that is no longer an option for me. Like my former wife would wisely say when she wanted to refrain from imbibing too much chocolate, "I just don't make it an option that I can consider. So, in a way, it's doesn't exist for me." Amen, I say to that—and for fear, as well.

Ask yourself this: in the larger context of giving meaning in your Life, why would you decide to do, or invest your Life in, something for which you had no enthusiasm? Why would you commit to something your heart is not in; something in which you do not feel alive; something for which you have no passion? Can you imagine anything worse? If you do not feel the enthusiasm or passion for a Life path, from your profession all the way to some relationship, do not go there. That is not your answer. Spiritually, the only real answer is to go for the *juice*! Go where the voice of enthusiasm and passion takes you. You will not be sorry. Nor will you ever be alone.

On the other hand, to reside in loyalty to our belief in ego betrays our Truth of Being. This is such a disservice to all we touch, as well as ourselves. Stuck in the unawareness of our sacred calling, we tend to serve others behind a mask that hides a false sense of unworthiness. In this framework we strive until we drop to serve everyone and anyone, and always at our own expense. In the final analysis we find only that we've used this external striving as a distraction, just so we won't have to look at our dysfunctional world within.

A friend once told me of a stunning discovery he made in this regard while engaged in an intensive spiritual-recovery retreat over a weekend. At a particular moment in a meditative state, an image came crashing through to him as divine revelation. He saw himself as a butterfly, flapping his wings furiously, hoping to keep the world going. In the wake of that image, he realized that he had been using the crutch of external purpose to fulfill his internal need. When we discussed it, he said to me in conclusion: "I finally got it that it's not my business to hold up the world. My only business is to fulfill my true Being, my Truth—for me. If I do just that faithfully, then I'll be so much better, not only because I'll be living with integrity, but that integrity will also nourish all my relationships and fulfill my purpose of Being." I'd say my friend got his money's worth out of that weekend, wouldn't you?

Ways of gnowing Truth

Acknowledging and celebrating the enthusiasm and passion we have for a particular aspect of Life, or even Life in general, is one good way of gnowing that the Truth has just surfaced and we are happy to be expressing it. Another way is by acknowledging that which comes to us in the silence of our Being. It is not that we have to take ourselves into a meditative state in order to gnow the Truth, although for many this can be and is helpful. The way I am talking about here is the voice we hear between the words and sentences spoken and read. If we listen carefully to what another is saying instead of preparing ourselves to make the next declaration, we will hear the voice of Wisdom speaking to us.

Truth also can be found in the silence from which speaks from a paragraph spiritually crafted or a brush stroke lovingly applied. By getting out of our own way, and letting go of the need to control everything, the Spirit can have its way with us.

By silencing ego consciousness we come to Truth. This is the voice to which we must become attuned, and of its fruit more fully aware. It is to this that we must surrender.

We all have heard this resonance with Wisdom speak within us. We might not identify it quite this way, or think that it's other than a choice to be made. That does not change the nature of Truth, however, or to what our sacred nature calls us. It is only ego consciousness that holds Truth as a choice, so the ego can have an equal chance to barter for your presence and activation on its behalf. The fact of the matter, however, is that ego is a mortal configuration or illusion crafted out of mass consciousness that has at its foundation the belief in the absence of, or separation from, the calling of Wisdom.

Through the use of this belief the ego establishes the idea, again and again, that we have a choice of whether or not to believe in God, and even whether it is God that is omnipotent, omniscient, omnipresent, and ever active. It is from this faulty premise that people fight to the death for their beliefs and opinions, when, spiritually speaking, beliefs and opinions are Self-limiting in their nature. It is only from our inner gnowing that we come to know that beliefs have nothing to do with spiritual fulfillment. Only experiencing our inner gnowing can provide fulfillment.

There is no mistaking the voice heard inwardly. It is soft, instantaneous, and absolutely delightful to behold. We call this gift by a number of names, depending on the slant we want to put on it. To begin with, we might well call this resonance or inner voice intuition. Intuition must be spiritual, if for no other reason than because those steeped in ego consciousness pooh-pooh intuition as a mere subjective, even sentimental, response to what Life brings us. And certainly inappropriate for real men to develop and use. Well, seeing as there really is no truly objective response because of our innate capacity for layering our history on all perspectives and perceptions, to deny the real meaning gained from our intuition strikes me as sheer folly, and as a misunderstanding of the nature of true gnowing.

Another term we could easily use to describe the transformative nature of Truth discerned is insight; and yet another, enlightenment. I like these terms for the light they bring to ignorance or darkness. Each reflects inner gnowing in the purest way, extended from the beacon of Truth—Wisdom—the Christ within each of us. And we are led beyond intellectual and emotional information and interpretation.

Then, of course, there's transformation and transcendence, and even resurrection. Each of these connotes a major yet sometimes subtle shift in meaning for the one who is paying attention with awareness. The shift is from a more material take on a particular matter to a spiritual relation. This sacred bond can then be utilized to shift not only one's comprehension of a situation, but also one's creative response to it, engaged and activated solely as the simple Truth. Truth's character is thus defined, bringing one's identity into congruence with that character. It is this we call home. For here we are relocated to the seat of our parenting, which sets our direction and purpose: the still, small voice of Wisdom. Indeed, we are comforted in the Truth of what we are. At last, we are at home with what we have found ourselves to Be: Wisdom continually and individually expressed.

This involves a genuine and complete commitment to The Inward Way. One day a friend sent me a glorious reminder of this necessary focus she found on a spiritual website: www.tut.com. It went something like this:

"It's not the dazzling voice that makes a singer. Nor clever stories that make a writer. And it's not piles of money that make a tycoon. It's having a dream and wanting to live it so greatly, that one would rather move with it, and 'fail,' than succeed in another realm. This is the pearl of great price you have chosen to follow.

At which point, of course, failure becomes impossible, joy becomes the measure of success, and fitting into the jeans you wore back-in-the-day, inevitable.

You so have what it takes, each of you!
The Universe."

Yes, service to your inner Truth is the highest form of Love. So focus on the pearl you are, and live true only to that!

Chapter Eight

Principle 6: Remembering to laugh at the idea of separation brings joy into celebrating the present

"Keep me from the wisdom which does not cry,
the philosophy which does not laugh,
and the greatness which does not bow before children."
Kahlil Gibran

The ultimate "cure"
One could easily respond to the forgoing principles by thinking they're just "too much" to take on. Truth be gnown, in a word, living spiritually is simple. By giving ourselves daily only to becoming and staying aware of the voice that speaks in silence, we express that resonance as our only commitment to Life. What keeps us from moving right out from the old habits into the new is the fear of what we might lose or become. Plus we think we have to undo all the past before we can fully live the Truth of Being.

This principle provides yet another vehicle that can both hasten our journey to spiritual fruition and relieve us of any burden in doing so. As a regularized way for dealing with any remnants of past error, let's look at Gibran's poetic commitment to spiritual living by translating it as we have Scripture. Here is one way to see it; you may have differing views that should be considered. This one is only to prime the creative juices:

"Keep me from the wisdom which does not cry," speaks to the depth of Truth that cries out to us, that beckons us to awareness and its expression. It is in the depths of Wisdom where the clearly profound "pearls of great price" are born, that cry out to us for completion.

"the philosophy which does not laugh," speaks to the way we usually treat what Life brings to us, and how we think about ourselves in that context: we take it, and ourselves, all too seriously. We give circumstances as well as our part in them way too much weight. The gravity of most circumstances and situations appears to be more than it really is, because when in ego consciousness we are self-absorbed. The world is not about us; it's only about delivering to the world the Truth heard in our hearts. Wisdom's deliverance opens us to the joy we find when we laugh at how seriously we've taken ourselves instead.

"and the greatness which does not bow before children." In the context of ego consciousness, greatness is usually thought to come from keen intellect or special talent and demonstrated in some kind of grand achievement. The greatness of which Gibran speaks is the greatness that bows in absolute humility to that which parents Wisdom into Being. Born out of innocence each sacred idea is an inspirational child born of Truth and is to be expressed in that image and likeness.

We have dealt with most of the elements of this marvelous testimony to Truth at great length. One that remains is to consider the place of laugher in living spiritually. What strikes me as strange about our current place in history is that laughter seems to be largely lacking. Fear has taken its place, rendering our ways far too somber to my liking. The heaviness of angst makes for an unbalanced lifestyle, where frowns replace grins of inner gnowing. It has almost gotten to the point where people do not even understand basic humor or irony as a way to release one from being overly serious about what surrounds and fills us these days. We seem to have forgotten to laugh, primarily at how seriously we have taken ourselves, as well as the false ideas of separation or duality that we have taken to be true. Indeed, we are heavily weighted down with the inconsequential and irrelevant.

Another thing that strikes me as strange is that nowhere in the Bible is there any direct reference to Jesus laughing. I would be willing to bet the family farm, if I had one, that Jesus must have enjoyed laughter immensely. My guess is that he used humor and irony a great deal as he interacted with the Pharisees, as well as in his other daily activities. He surely must have laughed, at lease inwardly, at the foolishness he encountered along his way. And he certainly did not take himself too seriously. Jesus bowed to the Wisdom found by regularly exercising humility.

Perhaps the writers of the Bible lived in times similar to our own. They certainly appear to have taken ego consciousness and the ways of separation from God way too seriously. All we need to return to for further clarification of this point is to remind ourselves that all but the first chapter of Genesis, plus Jesus' teachings, represents the ego's view of God and Life. Is it any wonder, then, that we find no references to laughter in Scripture? When buried in feelings of separation, guilt, and fear, there is not much to laugh at. One thing we gnow for sure: by living the Truth heard in silence, we are afforded *all* the gifts of the Kingdom, which do include laughter.

So what is the point? The point is that when we take ourselves too seriously, it means we take everything that happens in the context of self-importance. We put ourselves at the center of the Universe. We take whatever is said to or about us as if it were really true, or we defend against what appears to be false. The fact of the matter is that nothing said or done outside of us is the Truth about us in any way. The only Truth is what resonates as that in the silence Wisdom speaks. And Wisdom needs no defense. All else is a mistranslation. So what anyone else says about us or how we are to express what we really are is none of our business. What someone says about us is merely a reflection of how they see us. Such proclamations are only about their perceptions of us and not really about us. We can dismiss these simply by remembering not to take them seriously. Laughter is a good way to dismiss such illusions and set them free, along with the tension that has held them in place.

The only way another's view of us can be the Truth is when we are recognized for the individualization of the "I" we each are. And unless their acknowledgement comes from the "I" they are, it is still nothing but a projection of their perception. So, we might as well laugh at it, for the perpetrations of outer perceptions are humorous, even hilarious when compared to inner Truth. It is like saying we have a plan, derived out of ego consciousness. First of all, there is no such thing that can be fulfilled in any real way. Second, the only real design is to listen, moment to moment, for each direction toward fulfillment. Only Wisdom's Truth speaks that language.

In another sense, because most of us spend considerable energy dealing with memories of the past or dreams of the future we have little left that we can invest being in the present, the only place where Truth can be found. Ever wonder where the expression comes from that we use only ten percent of our brain? One answer I heard for this is that we use the other ninety percent dealing with gravity. Literally, such an explanation does not make a lot of sense. As a metaphor, however, it does make sense: we use ninety percent of our energy dealing with our perception of the gravity of day-to-day situations, when most, if not all, situations are only illusions thought to be true. Because we take such ego conscious renderings seriously, we expend considerable energy trying to figure them out or deciding how to deal with them. To take them seriously is to perpetuate missing the mark of spiritual reality.

Let us look carefully at what is being said here. Is anything from the past real in this present moment? Is anything you hope for, or fear repeating itself in the future, real right now? Of course not. Well, then, why do we spend so much energy contemplating either the past or the future? Why do we give past or future events power they do not, in and of themselves, have? Do any of the memories, glad or sad, or anything in between, have any real meaning? No, they do not, and yet we carry them along as though they do. Now, as more advanced spiritual Beings, we gnow we can see such things from a different perspective.

The admonition here is to take none of our memories seriously, for they are no more than illusions. No wonder we fail to see many smiles or much laughter; our faces and moods are too heavily burdened by the weight of seriousness we have placed on self-created mythology. The fact of the matter is that the past is history and the future is mystery. The present is now, so why take only now seriously and remember to laugh at the rest, while joy comes to our hearts by expressing the infinite array of gems from within?

The release

By artfully releasing illusions through laughter, we open the way for Truth to show its way. The more we engage with Wisdom instead of illusion, the more tension is released from our way of viewing Life. The more tension is released, the freer we feel to be true to ourselves. Thus, in this newfound bed of freedom to simply Be, we get to demonstrate the gifts of the Kingdom as we become aware of them. It is in this conscious awareness of all of the gifts of Wisdom that we find the joy we are. This Truth replaces the erroneous idea that we must work hard to find joy without. And it defines free will.

The same can be said for all the other attributes of divinity. It is not that we must strive to find or achieve them but that we are to express all we already are, which is the fullness of the infinitude divinity represents. At last, we find that we are indeed perfect, even as God is perfect. This is what renders us complete, even as others are complete. Thus we do not need to find someone or something outside ourselves to complete us. Rather, we share our completeness without any need to change anyone or any thing, and free all to be only what they are. What a Life-changing experience this is! Try it. You will like it, of that I am sure.

As a way to prime the laughter pump, you might try renting a few really funny movies and viewing them in the privacy of your own space. Do not anticipate or have any expectations. Those are the ego's way. Simply let yourself Be, without judgment of any kind. You will be amazed at the sense of humor lodged within you. I've been there, done that, and it has reaped great rewards. Opening myself to humor has gone so far that I have learned to let myself be spontaneous with it. Sometimes it seems that it just cannot wait to burst out of me. I had never thought of myself as funny until I let myself Be funny, and my sense of humor was verified by some friends. It is amazing what we find out about our real selves when we finally let ourselves simply Be centered in Truth.

Reading the "comics" section of the newspaper can also help. So can viewing some of the comedy on television. All may not suit you, which is fine. The only purpose is to open yourself up to the potential for laughter, so you can use it to release day to day tension. Believe me, you will soon view much of what you formerly would have taken seriously in a much lighter way. When you do, you will easily be able to laugh at what has no real meaning for you. It is at this point that you will be living in the now and enjoying every moment of it, and others will be highly encouraged to follow suit. Yes, the gift we demonstrate openly becomes one for more Universal purpose in a hurry. Laughter, like happiness, is contagious. And when we remember to laugh we are freed to live what we were truly created to Be. Then what we inherently gnow to be the Truth also comes to light.

Chapter Nine

Principle 7: I am my brother's brother, not my brother's keeper

"I am my brother's brother, not my brother's keeper."
The answer Jesus would have given if asked.

It is amazing how many have distorted Cain's answer to the Lord (Genesis 4:9) to mean that it *is* our life purpose to be our brother's keeper. Because it has been taught from the pulpit that this is so, religious leaders have verified this judgment by translating Jesus' acts to support their belief. From a spiritual foundation, however, when we charge ourselves with taking care of the needs of others we are shortchanging both them and ourselves from the beginning. We abuse their right to individual privacy as well as disrespecting their spiritual perfection. And we hold our own unique expression of Wisdom in abeyance. Each is an act lacking spiritual authenticity.

The only way that we can be our brother's keeper would be if we believed that our brother is separate from us. When grounded in ego consciousness, holding others to be who they are not, we hold others in bondage to their humanness. Wisdom's obligation is to hold all in the vision of spiritual awareness that individually expresses itself. When we see Life as individual expressions of the One, we come to see *that* as the only Truth. And we are honor bound to hold all *in* that Truth.

I am confident that if Jesus were asked if we were to be our brother's keeper he would have answered that we are not. Why would I say such a thing? Because the Bible is a series of allegories depicting essentially ego consciousness, if we were to be our brother's keeper we would be acting out of a sense of separation, not Oneness. Thus, to take care of our brother—seen as different and separate from us—is to imply that spiritual means can be used to heal physical disease or effect some other physical change. The emphasis on changing some condition external to us or healing someone separate from or different than we are conveys a statement grounded in ego consciousness.

On the other hand, when we see our brother in the same Light we are, all we need to do is hold all in that sameness of Truth, the Principle of spiritual Life. When we hold all, irrespective of appearance, in the enlightened spirit of Oneness, we are holding them in their perfection. This is how Jesus saw all, as One individualized—as brothers giving brothers the proper perception of divine consciousness, One as all. He saw no error where others saw humans as diseased physical entities. The best they could do in this context was to want to practice thinking spiritually. But until they witnessed their own Wisdom they could not act out of inner Truth, the Principle that holds all as perfect, even as God is perfect. One cannot serve spiritual consciousness and ego consciousness simultaneously. Either Oneness is the Principle by which we live and act or it is not. To keep the explanation of spiritual Life simple, each of us has only to answer and honor the still, small voice.

Through religious dogmestication many of us have learned to pray for others, even if they have no idea we are. We launch out, full force, thinking we can and should heal what ails them, as though our prayers could do such a thing. Yet, as we have learned earlier in this work, prayers do no such thing. The only real prayer is to live true to what we are. Living true to what we are does not include taking care of someone else, unless the Wisdom of the moment bids us to enter that arena. To pray for someone who has not requested it, or from whom we have not gained permission, is an invasion of privacy. This does not mean we should not offer our assistance when called for. In this case we then go inward for the best ways to serve the call. Following the call of Wisdom is precisely our purpose. However, there is a big difference between making ourselves into a martyr or exercising a messianic complex and simply following inner Authority.

The real task at hand

So far, we have come to the awareness that what we see outside us is only the appearance of what is not real—spiritually, that is. This being so, what is ours to care for? An illusion? The only thing to care for is our view of Life. When we are looking at Life from a perspective that appearance is to be dealt with, we are saying all found outside us is real and thus needs either to be enjoyed or fixed.

Spiritually, the only thing we can change is how we are viewing Life. This is our single task: discerning our current perspective and realigning it with spiritual Truth. Life becomes a never-ending commitment to shift perception, raising physical appearance to spiritual awareness at every turn. With practice we become more and more adept at this process until, at some point, it becomes routine. Just a glimpse of erroneous perception provides the impetus for transcendence. And we are born again into the awareness of Wisdom that is to guide us on our way.

One simple way to think about this process is think of a time when you became aware of a misspelled word in some book you were reading. Could you change the spelling of the word in the book? No, not really. You cannot magically shift the letters on a printed page to the correct way. What *can* you do about it? You can correct the spelling in your mind. The same is true for each and any error you see or hear elsewhere. Life is not about changing someone who does not speak, act or write to your point of view, no more than it is to fix someone's disease. Our only task is to correct inwardly what we are witnessing outside of us, so we walk forward with the deeper view intact. It is from this continuous commitment that we become more spiritually adept.

The same is true with any erroneous appearance we see or hear outside ourselves. When we see someone making the claim of disease, our only task is to see the perfection of that person instead. Inwardly, from the secrets conveyed by the voice of Wisdom, we can use the simple declarations when such error comes before us, like, "That's not God," or "God is perfect, and this appearance is not that." Having made the correction in our perception, we then simply move on without further ado. Surely we can respond to a call for help, but not if we are still holding onto the idea that someone who is already perfect somehow needs changing. If we respond to a call for help, our purpose is to hold the space of Truth for the one who calls upon us until they can shift their inner perception for themselves. In this way, they are led to transcendence by our example.

If you have ever been to the bedside of one claiming disease without buying into their claim, you surely saw their spirits lift in your presence. How could this be so? Just a few moments ago, as you entered, they were embedded in the belief of demise lodged in the diagnosis. Yet, by staying in your own perfection, and rendering that same perfection to the one making the claim—silently, within—they returned, even if only temporarily, to their Truth. This goes to show you that the example we set lifts all around us to that same level. Indeed, when we hold all in the Christ, in the Truth of their Being others cannot help but feel better, and even closer to that Truth themselves.

Spiritually, divine consciousness holds no maladies. Wisdom is free from all limitations, all misperceptions, and all erroneous thoughts, anything that is opposed to Oneness. Therefore, our purpose in this regard is to inwardly correct any allegiance to such error, any attachment to belief or opinion. When we leave such intact we are exercising a great disservice to mankind. It is our obligation to correct each erroneous appearance, so our example can lift the Universe likewise. This may seem like an impossible task, yet it is not. Just return to your enlightened state and you will recall that whatever we do to correct misperception is somehow correcting it for all. This is the only lifting we are to do, and we don't need to talk about it with anyone. Pray—that is, live—in secret, Jesus told us—demonstrate our inner calling of Truth secretly. Thus both disease and duality are eliminated from view.

When we share our inner connection openly, we betray its purpose. Our purpose is to commune with Wisdom and get out of our own way so it can flourish free from any ties to ego consciousness. To share this communion with another is to admit there *is* another when there is only Wisdom individualized. All "others" will automatically be lifted somehow, simply because they also are the One individualized. Besides, to do so could easily influence one not highly versed in spirituality to think we are using spirituality to shift human condition. We are not doing that. We are only abiding the awareness of the One..

On the other hand, if you are asked to teach about such things you should feel free to respond affirmatively—providing you are also demonstrating what you teach, walking your talk. When walking your talk from spiritual intention you are lending your Truth to inspire theirs. And it is from the spaciousness of the Christ within you that is connecting with the same in them that they will come to comprehend and live more fully their own.

When we look at the world this way, we are not overcoming any particular problem or looking for any particular favor. We are simply taking ourselves into a different dimension of consciousness. We can be conscious of physicality. We can take ourselves to another level of consciousness by seeing Life spiritually, and by using intellect to head in the direction to some new perspective. The ideal is to go even further, to the heart of Wisdom, where all is perfect, "even as God is perfect." By treading this path, we are not seeking to correct anything outside ourselves. It is amazing how problems thought to be real suddenly dissipate before our eyes. It is the natural outcome of living authentically.

Our purpose, then, is to maintain a sense of the voice of Wisdom; to shift outer appearance to inner reality; and to abort allegiance to outer authority in favor of abiding inner Authority. In this way we indeed die daily. We die regularly to outer appearance that forms as dis-ease, so that we carry Life disease-free through eternity. As long as we proceed on this path, we are continually freed from all that holds us from the awareness of our completeness. In spiritual consciousness any form of darkness is rendered obsolete. This is the function of enlightenment, after all.

I saw this on a bumper sticker one day: If God were everything to me nothing would bother me. "Wow," I wondered, "is this possible?" Yes, this is precisely what we are talking about here. If something is bothering me it is because I am seeing it for what it is not. I am seeing the appearance of it, and the dissonance I feel from giving some errant appearance power is notifying me of that fact. In each instance where this occurs it is a sure clue that I am to go within for corrective measures of some kind. The easy way to start this process of inner harmony is to remember not to take the dissonance too seriously. It is but one sure sign we are out of sorts with inner Truth. When we get past the idea that there are many alternatives for dealing with discord and come to apply only conscious awareness regularly, we will have arrived at home. When we have learned to stay in awareness, indeed everything absolutely *will* be as God or sacred consciousness to us. And, truly, nothing *will* bother us any longer. How could residing in Wisdom be bothersome?

The key here is to remember to practice conscious awareness all throughout the day, every day. We must persist if we are to be freed of all that has held us in the past, or of the fear of the past repeating itself. This process is not about being our own psychiatrist so we can clear every little piece of erroneous perception before we can be perfect. It is about practicing conscious awareness of our inherent Wisdom, which, in and of itself, frees us from any and all misperceptions. When we let up or feel we need a break from it all, not only are we letting ourselves down, we are obviating our spiritual commitment to the Universe. Each of us is called to Be only what we are, throughout eternity. By fulfilling this calling we honor both others and ourselves. Each aspect of our inner calling is for a more Universal purpose than just some selfish act.

This all may be true, but if not practiced or if ignored, it might as well not be true at all. Ignorance or laziness are not excuses for failing to respond to our inner calling. Once aware of this calling, it is ours to follow. Period. Indeed, each element of inner calling is to be exercised through humility. Humility is thus defined as getting out of our own way and giving ourselves to the language of the still, small voice. Living in Truth brings all who come in contact with us, even temporarily, to that same deep level of spiritual consciousness.

True, some around you may think you have "lost it," are following some weird spirit or voice of insanity. Their view matters not one iota. All that matters is that you are delivering Wisdom into the world; how another deciphers your demonstration of Wisdom is none of your business. No matter how they convey their feelings about your behavior, however, each is lifted in some measure to deeper meaning, even if only as a seed planted. In this way, we are indeed like Johnny Appleseed, who scattered apple seeds that others might flourish. Scatter your seeds of Wisdom, then, so what comes of the seeds will be laden with spiritual fruit.

Chapter Ten

Why Bother?

"This silence, this moment, every moment, if it's genuinely inside you, brings you what you need. There's nothing to believe. Only when I stopped believing in myself did I come into this beauty. Sit quietly, and listen for a voice that will say, 'Be more silent.' Die and be quiet. Quietness is the surest sign that you've died. Your old life was a frantic running from silence. Move outside the tangle of fear-thinking. Live in silence."

Rumi

If you have gotten this far, it is a sure bet you are willing to continue on the journey that is you. Perhaps you have picked up some pretty good reasons for wanting to do so, as well as ways for activating your newfound sense of Being. Yet, for many of us, having been stuck on the plane of ego consciousness for so long makes it seem difficult, if not impossible at times, to make the shift to The Inward Way. Be assured that even this slight hesitation is a sign that ego consciousness is still at work. This need not be a bad thing, for once we recognize ego consciousness for what it is—fear expressing itself, usually in the form of resistance—then we can move beyond fear to the Truth of our Being.

The crème de la crème

The crème de la crème of all this is that each of the seven principles is a means for becoming aware of, and casting aside, erroneous beliefs and opinions in favor of demonstrating only Truth.

As we use each of these principles, they will free us from

those illusory fragments that have haunted us, seemingly forever. Once the error—the belief, opinion, and/or feeling—is revealed, all we need do is embrace the spiritual sense of it. Do not think about or analyze the feeling or the language that has held that imagery in place up until now. Once revealed, all it takes for the long-held imagery to let go is sitting with its symbolic meaning until the erroneous view passes. This could take a few seconds up to a few days, but rarely longer. True, it could resurface as yet another layer later on. Just repeat this simple exercise if it does.

Thus we engage the meaning of the admonition to stop, look, and listen. Stop whatever you are doing at the moment the image or feeling strikes you; look at what you discern symbolically, not literally, listening within for its meaning for you. Once you have discerned the meaning through your resonance with the Truth you hear, that image and feeling will simply drift away and leave you feeling light as air, and bright as the noonday sun. Doing more than this is to take you, and your feelings, beliefs, and opinions way too seriously. Just remember to laugh, and the tension that surrounds dysfunction will ease, releasing untruth into the ethers.

As you will remember, Principle One deals with becoming aware of what you are, so you can let go of all those false images of who your ego thinks you are—so your real identity can be restored to the Truth of your Being. As you let go of those erroneous self-perceptions of you, your spiritual identity will show its face as the face of Spirit, the Truth of the Christ you are. This constitutes the resonance you hear and feel as Wisdom is revealed to you. Then, sometime along the way of Life, you will come into the sudden awareness that you are spiritual and not material; whole and complete, and not in need of something or someone to complete you; perfect in the eternity and immortality of your Being; and free from suffering the underlying fear of disappearing upon physical death. Free from judgments of those who as yet do not gnow the ways of Truth, and who instead join the mass consciousness means of inflicting wounds through flaw identification.

Principle 1 will initiate the process of cleansing the unwanted, and will do so without any great effort on your part. All it will take is awareness in combination with surrendering to the Wisdom you hear. And letting go of all the rest, as if sending a basket of woes—those which many of us have erroneously considered to be our treasures in some way—into the Universe, never to be seen or bothered by again.

Now that you gnow the Truth of your spiritual Being, Principle 2 simply focuses on the admonition to stay in the Truth that speaks within you as your moment-to-moment guide. Once aware, and practiced, soon you will express Life unencumbered by any false images. Instead, your days will be filled with the gifts of the Kingdom, and you will be celebrating them as though you always had.

This feature of a principled Life makes you free to live the Truth of what you are with integrity. Soon enough you will see that Life is only a matter of obedience or surrender, and not one of working your way past the seeming trials and tribulations formerly thought to be true. Thus you are freed on yet another plane of existence, moving deeper and deeper into the fullness of your Being.

Principle 3 deals activating Truth. Those who already are in touch with their inner Being gnow that spiritual demonstration does not come out of intellect. It is mimicking that comes out of intellect, but real demonstration is more than a thousand kisses deep. It comes out of a deeply passionate connection within us, where true freedom has its way with us.

We can learn intellectual approaches for various forms of physical creation, but those only reflect the more "technical" approaches to brush stokes, imaging, shaping, and shuttling. The results of such renderings can be quite spectacular to the physical eye, but somehow they just lack "soul." They fail to speak in the tongue of Spirit, and instead leave us technically pleased but soulfully empty. The requisite heart connection simply is not made, cannot be made, utilizing the intellect alone.

When we let Truth have its way with us in all facets of its demonstration, we are giving impetus for the fullness of Life's meaning to quicken the hearts of those who are open to the Way of the Christ each is. In this way—having gotten out of our own self-important way, that is—we will have shed the false idols: cast them away, in favor of letting ourselves just Be with all that is. The result, as you well gnow by now, is that we will have deepened our spiritual awareness. From this deeper understanding we see that spiritual demonstration is nothing but our Truth activated into the Universe, to be enjoyed by those who are aware and ready to be "touched" by it.

Principle 4 speaks to the application of the faith *of* God being the key to spiritual fulfillment. Applying this principle can awaken us to our undying commitment to activate spiritual Life into Being. Here again we find that divine Authority or Wisdom governs real Life, whereas outer authority only provides us with food that might fit our fancy but not the inspiration that calls to us.

This letting go, forgiving old beliefs about a god external to ourselves—and the ways in which the fear of ultimate separation expresses the idea of pain and suffering—brings us to yet another validation of our spiritual connection as One with all, never to be forgotten. Practicing this principle will eventually make us free from all those past ways of habitually exercising ego consciousness in order to gain something that can neither make us happy nor bring us peace—or that will last beyond the next infatuational rendering of material desire.

Principle 5 speaks to the highest form of Love. For how long have we on this plane of ego consciousness exercised all else but the Truth of our Being? Do not "hear" this as a criticism. I phrase it this way only to point out that—for most of us, much of the time—we have been driven by collective consciousness expressed through the neediness of the ego form. How, then, could we be expressing the highest form of Love? Most assuredly, we can from time to time exercise what we'd normally classify as loving acts. The ego conscious concept of love gives way to a new perspective: only the Truth of our Being opens us to the Way of Loving that stems from spiritual authenticity. When we exercise spiritual authenticity into all phases of Life, we will be nothing but what we are: Love individualized and individuated.

It is in this image and likeness of God that we Love simply and effortlessly. By staying true to our spiritual identity, we express the fullness of passion and enthusiasm for Life, including compassion for all around us, as well as ourselves. How much more can Love Be than this? Surely racing through the planet in the fast lane cannot hold a candle to this level of Being. This sacred way frees us to Be only what we already are — perfections of Being — through all we do. Thus, when steeped in the awareness of the Christ, we give only the crème de la crème we each are to the Universe. Indeed, this is living authentically. And there is nothing like it! Of that can you be sure.

Principle 6 deals with not taking ourselves so seriously, the cure for much that troubles us in the realm of ego consciousness. This awareness releases us from dis-ease with all the unfound weightiness we carry around. Most of all this is illusion, and when we can laugh at our serious take on illusion we are freed to live all we are, instead of living mostly the limitations we have placed on ourselves. Laugh it up. Let people think you're crazy. Soon they will get the method of your madness and join in. It is then that the masses will begin letting go of their illusions, too, and we will be well on our way to the Universe of Truth we actually are. We will be returning to the full awareness of Wisdom, and living more and more from that.

Principle 7 speaks to our real place as holders of Universal Truth. It is our natural form of Wisdom that commands our awareness. As we stay in that awareness, all are lifted somewhat to that same level. Thus we are not to be our brother's keeper but our brother's brother, his equal in every spiritual way. As we stay in that awareness, each with whom we come in contact is led to that same Truth within their own heart. At least at some level of Being, they truly resonate with Truth and are thus comforted by it. Who would not be when resting in the lap of luxury? The spiritual way is luxurious, and we feel deliciously at home when we gnow that to be the only Truth for us.

And so it is

What else needs to be said to convince you that Life as a "speed bump" is much richer and more authentic than living in the "fast lane?" When we allow ourselves to slow down enough to hear the Truth spoken in the silence between the raindrops and the breaths that separate words shaped in voice or written form, we will hear the Wisdom which informs Life with all the riches of the Kingdom. Surely, we can see by now that these spiritual riches are not to be found in some belief held in ego or collective consciousness.

Now then, what is left to decide, to choose? If you are still clinging to the idea of choice it is a sure bet that you are stuck in some level of ego consciousness. Life is not about a choice to see the Truth or not. Neither is Life about learning anything new. Life is about remembering what you are, sacred essence, and living true only to that. Shakespeare said to us: "To thine own self be true," and it was never more relevant or inspiring. Yet, in the fullness of the Truth it holds, it might better be conveyed as: To thine own Self, Be your Truth.

Silence your own thoughts, your worries and fears. Silence your beliefs and opinions. In the spaciousness of Wisdom, let Life have The Inward Way with you in the fullness of awareness and remembrance. THIS is living spiritually. Celebrate living spiritually as your only Truth, for indeed it is. Indeed, so you are! And Wisdom reigns.

Being on your way

Below you will find for each of the seven principles suggestions for applying what has been unleashed in the explanation for each principle. It is one thing to comprehend the deeper meaning of Life. It is yet another to activate that meaning into your everyday Life. Being is the activation that takes you from the static realm to the active one, from just thinking about your essence to demonstrating what you really are. Being what you are is your new way, the way of living only from the seat—and seed—of Wisdom.

Chapter III, Principle One: When you become fully aware of *what* you are, you will be what you really want to see.

It is said that it takes practicing a new habit—in this case, seeing Life from a metaphysical perspective—something like forty days in order to shift from the old way. Of course, something may already have struck from within you to suit this purpose, so by all means go with that. If not, perhaps something from what follows will prompt just the right way for you.

When we come to the awareness of *what* we are, so that can replace all the false beliefs and opinions relating to *who* we think we are, we are suddenly thrown into a whole new mindset about Life and our place in it. We finally come to the awareness that corresponds to our "what-ness," the ever-growing expression of our divinity. Once aware, we will have unleashed the Truth of our Being and this Truth is the most powerful cause available to us. There are not two powers, two causes, remember—only One—and this is the divine each of us already is.

The difficulty with moving forward in this new meaning of Life for us is not that we have to learn a new lesson over and over again, finally to learn what we are. Rather, it seems difficult because we do not *remember* that we are *what* we are. Mired in duality a while yet, the ego renders things spiritual to be easily forgotten.

Here is a way to break that phase of ego consciousness called forgetfulness. The word Namasté, pronounced NammaSTAY, is a Sanskrit greeting with deeply spiritual meaning. The surface meaning of Namasté says, "I greet the divine in you." For those who have taken it to the depths of Truth, however, the meaning comes to be: "As a divine Being, I acknowledge and celebrate the fullness of your divinity."

The distinction is a good one to consider for a moment. To hitch one's Life to the former is to keep one in separation by acknowledging only the divine *in* them. It is like acknowledging someone as a lung or kidney because they have one or more of these in them. Just how shallow is that? The real test of divinity comes to roost in the totality of Being, and the totality of our Being rests in divinity. We *are* divinity individualized; remember? Divinity expressed as Wisdom, and nothing but that.

So what does Namasté have to do with remembrance of our divinity? The suggestion here is to practice greeting everyone and everything with a soft and gentle, even silent—but with absolute conviction and intention—Namasté. It will also be helpful if you somehow write out the word Namasté on little pieces of tape or paper and affix them to the most prominent places in your daily contacts, like the refrigerator, bathroom mirrors, and your car rear-view mirror; even on the face of your computer and the screen of your TV. On each, place this holy greeting and spiritual Truth in a space most conspicuous to your view. Each time you see it, say it to yourself—and take on its meaning as the Truth about you. Say it as you brush your teeth, as you open your computer, as you look in your rear-view mirror before you put your car in gear. Say it every time you see someone (even a tree or squirrel) approaching. If you are hesitant at first to do this, merely say it silently, but say it, nonetheless. Every time!

The key is not so much the acknowledgment of divinity through words. It is the full awareness of divinity brought about by acknowledging another person or thing as divine with the fullness of conviction Oneness exemplifies. Change begins with the conscious awareness of a new way, and eventually the awareness fills you to the brim, freeing you to express this awareness to one and all without even thinking about it. In this process not only does the one greeted with Namasté get to be reminded of, and be nourished by, the Truth of their Being, the greeter is also fed by the affirmation of his own divinity each time he expresses it thus.

A second suggestion: every time you hear or see yourself saying something, or behaving in a way counter to your divinity, say Namasté to yourself. This is an excellent correctional device that reverses the "anti-Christ," or "anti-divine" aspects that creep back into our day-to-day situations and circumstances from time to time. Just keep in mind that every time you hear yourself act in some way contrary to your divinity you are propelling yourself and all the energy of the universe in a direction opposite to your Truth of Being, the opposite of Wisdom. In order to reverse this direction, it takes only a reaffirming commitment to the ever-present awareness and acknowledgment of our divinity in common. This is the absolute "cure" of all that ails us in our misunderstanding of what we really are.

You might want to say something like, "I Am divine, and in my divinity I call to bear on my Life all that is good, for I am only good and manifest all I see as That, good." The key is to develop a quick awareness of straying away from what is divine, and to then reverse it with the Truth. When we take such positive action, once again we unleash all the power available to us as divine Beings. Indeed, divine is *what* we are. As we claim only this Truth, all the rest is given unto us.

Chapter IV, Principle Two: Being and staying in spiritual awareness determines what is real.

Accepting ourselves as "perfect" can be difficult at first, but with practice this divine reality can become second nature. Actually, it will result in a return to our *only* nature: perfectly divine. We can be reminded of our perfection of Being in many ways. For example, all of us have "resonated" with some Truth between the words or lines of a particular written piece. The same is True in oral communication. Practice listening very carefully to what others are saying and refrain from the inner chatter that is wanting to rejoin the other before he or she has completed a sentence. My friend Margy calls this inner urge, as well as the meaningless casual chatter about others, "matter chatter," for it has no real value for us as we fully engage with Life from the conscious awareness of Wisdom.

More to the point, just plain listen, not so much even to the words. Concentrate on the spaciousness between the words, the pauses that give us space in which to hear the Truth in our hearts, the resonance if you will, that makes us gnow its special meaning. Quite frequently it won't even be in the same ballpark of what another is saying, for the resonance we hear is only for us.

What comes to us in the fullness of spiritual intimacy called silence is the Christ, our inner presence speaking in a voice we can now hear. To share such revelations with another is perfectly fine, even if these do not directly benefit them. The real help, however, is that you are serving as an example for them to listen to that still, silent voice within themselves, and this can serve them equally well. What a gift of divine friendship this is! Surely, Wisdom lends us to one another this way.

Yet another helpful practice is to be watchful of our feelings. This need not be an arduous, overly detailed approach at all. It is only about paying attention to what feels "right" to us in any given situation. We also know when some thing, circumstance, or thought just does not feel "right" to us. We have all had such things trip our emotional triggers. When we feel anything counter to our own divine "goodness," it is only a matter of acknowledging such feelings and then installing the Truth in their place.

This suggestion is all about developing a sense of "watchfulness," and "watchfulness" does not contain one shred of judgmental labeling in it. Watchfulness is merely a state of sufficient detachment from a thought or act to see it simply for what it is. Either it is Loving or it is not, and none of it needs to be labeled in any way for whatever it is. It is only what it is, and its meaning can be neutralized when we are not so attached to it that we feel the need to defend it. If your behavior does not demonstrate loving, merely listen to the inner voice of Wisdom and change the thought or action to one that is Loving.

Living from the nonjudgmental nature of Truth frees us from being held hostage to such false demands. In Truth we find that both forgiveness and apology are meaningless. Either is but a veil for hurt feelings or coming from a perspective of victimization. In this deeper sense we come to see that forgiveness is tantamount to seeing Life from the perspective of Truth instead of our belief in separation or duality, and we no longer hold anyone hostage to correct something that only we can change for ourselves.

In this way, too, we are making a friend, or at least a helper, of what ego consciousness mirrors to us. Through detached awareness we see ego consciousness presenting us with an example of that which is not the Truth. As we practice viewing our day-to-day existence in this light, we can see that these reflections alert us to the necessity of dismissing them at first sighting. We see the false witness and respond with the nimbleness of a first-rate fire department in the heat of fire. Immediately we respond to the "alarm" our belief in duality represents. Through this discernment we act quickly and confidently to reverse it, so Truth may indeed prevail.

Actually, we are not reversing anything outside us at all. What is really happening in such shifts of meaning is that we are becoming aware once again. And we reinvest in spiritual awareness instead of allowing ourselves to put our trust in two powers. When we gnow the difference between the real and the unreal, why would be continue to chose that which is not?

The final suggestion related to this principle deals with finding happiness and peace. First of all let us remind ourselves, metaphysically speaking, that peace refers to peace of mind, free from the frame of mind that feels like a rattling cage of playful monkeys that can never be brought under control. Before looking at happiness, let us practice looking outside ourselves to see what could possibly—from the outside—fix this frame of mind. Think hard about it. Sorry for tricking you. Thinking hard about anything and everything is precisely what breeds and feeds "monkey-mindedness."

The never-ending search for the whys and wherefores of our daily existence is what characterizes the over-analytical manner in which ego consciousness works. What is the way out of this? We just need to practice being aware of our inherent Wisdom every time we find ourselves wanting direction. Going without is like going to a gasoline station for a new dress or a filet mignon dinner. Just how foolish is it to search for something where it cannot be found? Going outside to find spiritual meaning that is found only in our divinity is no less foolish. Practice practical Wisdom instead. Truth just is, and is always present for us, just waiting for us to show up in earnest.

Chapter V, Principle Three: Divine demonstration is the result of Truth activated.

You may well find it stimulating to follow your journey from day to day, just to see what it is that has been inspiring you. Is your demonstration initiated from some outside influence, or from the voice you hear within, as an "aha," some resonance felt, an inner gnowing that this is the Truth for you to follow? It pays to discern the difference, for what you use as your starting point is what determines the fruitage at the end of the day.

In an easy, unhurried way, just take a look at where you find yourself: mostly in your head, intellectually and personally; or seeing things differently, mentally; or coming from the inner authority of Truth. Once you gnow the difference the rest comes easily. Then it is all about pointing your feet—that is, your conviction and commitment—in the direction of the spiritual way that is your authentic Life expressed. From then on simply go with the flow, correcting your passage when necessary—and without judgment—and Life will change dramatically for the better.

At first, surrendering is a difficult, even scary, concept to understand and exercise faithfully. I used to say that spiritual Life is about being obedient to the inner callings of Truth, but too many people object to being obedient to almost anything these days, let alone Truth. It is simply too offensive, especially in a society which suggests that women should obey their husbands.

Surrendering need not be scary idea. All it really means to surrender is to exercise a willingness to follow the path we *really* want—divine consciousness—rather than the one we have been led to believe is the only way for us: ego consciousness. This is largely because of the supposed material wealth the latter can bring us. Yet, when we come to our spiritual senses we see the Truth above the din of material existence and we gnow without a shadow of doubt that this is the way for us.

So, as you practice observing yourself in everyday conditions and circumstances, listen for these designations of inner peace and joy, the extension of passion and compassion, and the expression of an easy enthusiasm for Life. These will tell you that you are in absolute harmony with divinity. When they are lacking, it is a sure sign that you are in line with some false idols instead. Once we feel the Truth that commands us to that way, the false impression of choice related to any other way soon disappears from view. Watch and adjust; watch and adjust; watch and adjust. Stay detached from what you observe and your emotions won't take control over your Life. Instead, Life will come to you as you never before have witnessed or celebrated. The time is now. The place is right here, within the depths of your heart.

As you observe your behavior throughout the day, discern if you are working hard at what you feel you are to do, or if it comes easily through you. If you are finding that your everyday happenings are feeling more like chores than fun, then more than likely you are exercising the parameters of work established by the collective consciousness and exercised through ego consciousness. Being a "hard worker" is the ego's way. After all, says the ego, we can hardly get to Heaven unless we prove ourselves on every level of behavior. On the other hand, if you are demonstrating your day from the center out by listening for the Wisdom that guides you only to your highest good, then in all likelihood your day is sailing by with ease. It will also be filled with the peace of Mind that is the only natural way for you, and with the joy that fills your heart in the ease of that goodness.

Finally, listen to the magnificent, inspirationally divine ideas that come through to you each day. Make a list of them as they occur and see what they feel and sound like to you. As long as they came to you from within, seemingly out of nowhere, they are gifts to be cherished and expressed with all the giftedness you have at your disposal—which is more than you can imagine. Just being aware of these gems of Wisdom is enough to assure you of their validity for you.

As you view each inspiration, make a commitment to complete every one of them. Do not leave a single one out as lacking some special "punch" for you. Such gifts are to be utilized to their fullest, as divinely created gifts to the Universe. Talk about an exciting Life to express! And you will not even have to work hard to make someone else happy with you, for your newfound happiness will be so obvious that no outside force will be able to penetrate your brilliance. Such is Life in the right lane.

Chapter Six, Principle Four: Expressing the faith of God is the key to spiritual fulfillment.

Being on your way corresponds to living metaphysically, living from the Truth of your Being. Thus, a Life lived in divine consciousness Truth is the Way in which one defines his or her Life. This is the Way, the Truth and Life of which Jesus spoke. If you want to return to this as your way, the only natural way spiritually, then what is required is a clear look at how we define God. Most of us define God in terms way too small, and thus we limit what God can and will do for us as simple reflections of what we think is important to us in the moment. Most assuredly, this places God outside us and diminishes the infinite power of divinity to such a degree that we miss most of what would be available to us when we are fully. Just substitute the idea of Wisdom for the word and idea of God and the full comprehension of spiritual Life will suddenly shift for you.

Take all the wraps off your definition of God and allow, even for just this exercise, the possibility that you, as God, are actually Wisdom individualized. And that you and God are truly as One. Take out a pad and your favorite writing instrument, or use your word processor if that works better for you. Split the page vertically down the middle. Now, on the left hand side of the page write down the definition of God you had before you picked up this book. Opposite that write the description of you before we began this journey together. Look at them very carefully and discern how they are different and the same.

Go within now. Breathe deeply a few times in order to release the tension, both from your day and from engaging this exercise. When you feel comfortable and at ease simply ask to be shown the real God, experienced as the voice of Wisdom. Be patient and let all the thoughts that arise and scatter through your brain go, waiting for an "ah-hah" moment to inform you of the Truth for you in each case. Then inscribe the answer you receive under the former definition of God on the left hand side of the paper.

Now, take a few more moments and repeat the exercise, but this time ask to be shown the real you. Just as before, let the monkey-mind have its way, letting it all pass through. Remember that you're not asking your brain to figure this out; you're waiting for Truth to show the way for you. Very soon now you will receive what you need to gnow. Write the spiritual response down under the earlier answer, on the right side of the page.

Staying in the same spiritual attitude, permit the Truth to be spoken as you discern the differences between your first answers and those that have arrived through spiritual discernment. Which feel "right" to you? Which do not? Ignore the urge to analyze each, for that will only take you to the means available through ego consciousness and forestall the Truth from speaking, from resonating within. Simply listen for the Truth between the sound of your heart beats; Wisdom is there, awaiting only your awareness.

Make note of anything that comes to you as Truth and then step away from it all for a few minutes. Release any tension you may feel in your body; release any thoughts that race through your mind. Stay in the spaciousness of the Spirit, the Christ you are. You will know you are there if your mind is at peace and you feel light-hearted. What you are hearing as Truth may well excite you, and that is a form of excitement that shows itself as enthusiasm for the Truth you have found.

Now look at what you have recorded. Gnow that this is the Truth your divine consciousness has given you. Trust it. Surrender to it. Follow it. Let it guide you on your way, always. Any time you find yourself other than where your Truth resides, merely return to the Wisdom you have just witnessed. Practice this regularly and, soon enough, you will rest in this conscious awareness more often than not. It will not be long before you are experiencing Life from this spiritual foundation alone.

Another exercise to consider is to write a letter to God, and another to you. See what you say in each. Discern whether you have separated yourself from either. If you have, you are functioning out of ego consciousness. If you see that you are as One with both you are functioning clearly out of spiritual integrity. If you are still part way in between, simply keep surrendering to the Truth you resonate with and soon you will be back where you belong. All the debris from a life of ego consciousness will be cast aside like a heap of fallen leaves sailing with the autumn winds.

After you have discerned which state you are in, if in the ego state I suggest you write a letter to God and you from the deeper meaning that you truly are One in Being. In this letter express what meaning this Oneness has for you, and how you see it demonstrating its Oneness in your Life. There is no right or wrong here, only the Truth that awaits your awareness so it can be activated and individualized as you. Just let it have its way with you and see where it goes. Put no restraints—no limitations—on it, whatsoever.

Consider for a moment what faith means to you. This is not a test to see if you recall the various approaches to faith offered earlier. It is merely taking a "look see" at how you are defining your spiritual Life. Again, there is no right or wrong. This is about discernment only, not about being judgmental toward yourself. After you have looked at your current definition of faith, return once again to the safe haven within and ask to see the Truth about faith; record it just as you have the others. Drink this new meaning in with all you are. Let it fill you to the brim, at all levels of Being. Even let it overflow if it must. Let it etch itself on the lining of your heart. Then simply rest in it and see what that feels like. Go there any time you feel that you've somehow separated from it. Wisdom is that accessible to you. It embraces you in all your splendor, and in all your opulence.

You may be tired of writing by now, but bear with me for just one more exercise that could well benefit you. Write down some of your favorite and/or most frequently used prayers. Do not think about them; simply record them. When finished, return to your definition of God and you. As you ponder those two, ask to be shown the form of prayer that now fits with those descriptions. Resist the temptation to figure this out in your head. Once again, simply let the Truth come from within you and record it as such. Sit with the response that comes up and let it come to the fullness of spiritual meaning for you. Once you have become aware, gnow this is Truth for you. Trust it. Surrender to it. Live from it. Be it, for you already *are* it. You always have been and always will Be the Truth you are, no matter what you think to the contrary.

Chapter Seven, Principle Five: Service to our inner Truth is the highest form of love.

This series of suggestions require very powerful commitment to envisioning the actual intention behind your behavior. Please— please—do not over-analyze what you do and think. All it takes to see the Truth for you, as opposed to that which is not, is simple discernment: a quick and simple looking within for the resonance that affirms Truth heard and activated.

Take a few moments to list the ways you express love to your family and friends, in the workplace, and at play. Just set the list free, don't over-think or stress over it; let this be a fun exercise, letting the examples just come out without the encumbrance of worry over whether you are a real "Lover" or not.

Once the list feels complete, just sit with each example and ask if this is a sign of authentic Love as you have expressed it. If it is, you will know it without a shadow of doubt, for it will match in kind the intention that flows naturally out of The Inward Way— of expressing only the Truth of what you are to all. Being sincere in your desire for spiritual honesty and integrity of Being, the list will sort itself out very nicely. Remember, you are the only one who will be reviewing this list, so do not be afraid to be absolutely truthful about it.

What do you do with the answers that do not "make the grade" of authenticity? Surely you do not want to punish yourself for such inauthentic renderings. All that is necessary is to see how they can be modified in order to engender a sure affirmation and validation of their spiritual worth. Then, just sit with the ones that you have shifted and let them write themselves on the lining of your heart. Soon you will be expressing these revised perceptions just as faithfully, and with complete integrity, as all the other demonstrations of the Loving way that you most naturally already incorporate into your daily Life.

Take a few moments now to sort out the times and places—and with whom—you have not really told the Truth about what you think and feel; about what you are really like in a relationship, and what you would like out of one that is genuine; about what you really want from Life; about what your real purpose of Life is and how you would like to fulfill that purpose—about that one thing that lies dormant within, waiting the simple awareness and commitment to authenticity in order to manifest as the gift you are to the world.

Once again, these are not exercises to make you feel guilty about not living the Truth of your Being. No one else will see this rendering but you, so be absolutely frank and honest with yourself. You will know if you are being truthful or not by the feeling you will have in the pit of your stomach or in the stirrings of your heart. I am speaking about the feelings you have about what you can and cannot stomach, and those you have from the stirrings of your devotion to Wisdom.

Added to this listing is your sense of how your actions in this regard could have affected your relationships: whether or not your loved ones really gnow you and what you really are like, and how you feel about Life and your place in it. Just coming to these realizations is the deepest and most honest form of intimacy, for by fathoming the depths of your Being you are placing yourself in touch with the real you, your Highest Self. It is now that you can be "real," instead of projecting a personality developed to protect you from all that troubles you, and as your way of handling Life from the seat of vulnerability.

Vulnerability is a sure sign of fear coming through to announce the lack of ease you feel with Life, a sense of distrust in the outcomes to follow, fearing that some unruly or unpleasant past will once again rear its head. It takes courage to face these feelings honestly. Once honored, you can walk through these feelings gnowing that you will find Truth on the other side. You will have the sudden and complete discernment that Wisdom is all there is. And that fear is nothing but a self-propelled illusion, the purpose of which is to keep us trapped in the web of ego consciousness.

That was the easy part, or so it will seem. Now that you have discerned the Truth for you, it is time to render this Truth out into the daily world in which you manifest that Truth. GULP! Yes, this can be scary at first, but just remember that "scary" is just another relative of abject fear, and must be faced and trod through to the other side, where Truth reigns supreme. So why not begin with something simple, like looking at your workstation on a spiritual level. Is this really what you want to be doing as your Life's calling? If not, then begin by taking the first step to change what you must Be, in order to live authentically.

Seek out ways of preparing more fully, if not already so, for the new path you know to be the Truth for you. Follow up to be sure you have what you need to be successful in this new realm of Being. Be assured that once you have declared your Truth with all you are that the Universe will show its face by providing all you will need to he highly successful. You just need to take the first step, and you'll be shown the rest of the way, including all the provision you will need to move on filled with enthusiasm for Life.

This is the Power of Truth declared, and in this divine declaration you will have unleashed the full power of the Kingdom that you have at your command. People and things and ideas will show up in ways that will surprise and delight you, all of which will carry you forward in all appropriate ways.

Next, you will want to share this newfound path with family and other loved ones. True, it might be a shock to some, yet your Truthfulness will also inspire others to their own Truth, which is part of our spiritual purpose of Being. Once another is moved to see the spiritual nature of your demonstration, it gives them permission to venture out in a similar way. In this sense, as we live our Truth we also are teachers for others who come into our path. For some, it may be just as a seed planted or as a bump in the night; for others, it will be a huge shift of perception.

For a time, relationships could be set ajar. This temporary shift in insight may have seemed to be a solid relationship could cause loved ones to be threatened at first, but once they see the spiritual Truth involved, all concerned will either embrace the new path or move on in another direction. Do not let the possibility of the latter happening discourage you from living your Truth. Remember to ask yourself this: "Why would I want to live with someone who did not want my Truth for me and have my best interest at heart?" Of course, the same applies to their way of being, should they be the ones initiating change.

Even though some may think you have gone off the deep end, let that not discourage you. As a matter of fact, let such happenings affirm the correctness of your new way. The way of Truth engenders a Life which will put off many, but mostly in a way that will shift them to some level of Being that is important to them. They might not gnow this at first, but that does not mean that you should not do what you must do. As you extend this activation of Truth for you into other areas of Being, you will see that not only are you a very different person, but those around you will be inspired beyond your wildest dreams for them. This, too—besides the Truth you are now expressing your authentic sense of Self—is a blessing for all who enter your path.

Often we make decisions about what we say and do in Life out of the influence of the collective consciousness of those around us, out of that seeming voice of linear rationality that wants us to believe that it is the Truth for us. Now is the time for you to break that mould, and express in its stead that which is sure to be the Truth for you. Take some time to list those things you sense are important for you to do. Now, as before, take this list within, and ask for a clear sign for those items that are the Truth for you. It often works best when we discuss such things with a trusted friend who will listen without judgment, simply providing feedback when asked. For example, if you are feeling the need for a transition into a new career path, list for your friend those possibilities that interest you, at least on the surface. Ask your friend to listen for the kind of energy you are expressing when discussing each possibility. You will find, I am sure, that with some items on this list you are being flat in your demeanor and level of enthusiasm. With others you perk up, have some positive energy toward. With still others, or perhaps only for the one real choice for you, your passion and enthusiasm for it will shine, will burst forth spontaneously. It is this one that is speaking in the voice of authenticity for you, that validates its Truth by being "in the presence of God," congruent with Wisdom heard. It is this one that is calling out to you for activation with the fullness of commitment you have, called the faith of God. It is this one that must be fulfilled if you are to live—that is, Be—in harmony with your Truth. Yes, you can come to the same authentic conclusion by simply going within for the answer to the same question and waiting for the response. The answer may not come right away, or it may come as a series of alternatives coming up one after the other that show you your lack of enthusiasm and passion for them. Either way, you get what you ask for, so begin now by asking the right question, always for the Truth of your Being. "I wonder..." is all you need ask, and the answer is there for you. Putting out the "I wonder..." is telling your Highest Self that you want to be made aware of the Truth for you, and once beckoned, Wisdom is sure to show its face. The same is true whether you want to inquire about a new career, relationship, place to live, whatever. It is all the very same, a willingness to become aware of Truth for you, so that you can activate that Truth as your divine consciousness individualized. So Be It! "Amen," I say to that.

Chapter Eight, Principle Six: Remembering to laugh at the idea of separation brings joy into celebrating the present.

As suggested in Chapter Eight, you might try renting a variety of funny movies, gauging your sense of humor as you view them. The same is true about sorting out which of the comic strips in the Sunday newspaper tickle your funny bone. Still another way is to view some sit-coms on TV, sorting out which make you laugh. It also pays to give attention to others' use of humor. Hang around people whom you find funny; they are there to put you in touch with that piece of you that you have been denying. My bet is that you are more humorous than you think you are. When living mostly from a basis of ego consciousness we take Life and ourselves all too seriously, and this becomes a serious limitation on the real us.

All this is to say that there is a great deal of humor in Life, contrary to what we see around us these days. There is humor in most everything that presents itself to us. It is just that we are unaccustomed to seeing it. Humor will help provide the awareness that we *are* humorous—at least most of what we take so seriously is that. When we can learn to see Life from this new perspective, we will be well on our way to laughing our way into the Truth of Being.

The real key is to set ourselves free from taking both ourselves, and much that we think about, so seriously. Most of what we think about relates to the past or future, thus keeping us from the present moment, the only one moment we can live. Neither God nor we are in the past or future. We are here only now. Each time you find yourself thinking about the past or future, remember to laugh, meaning not to take it seriously. Why should we take the past or future seriously when it is nothing, no thing, at all? Joel Goldsmith admonishes us to "nothingize" such thoughts, make no thing of them, for they are not real.

Also, you might want to practice laughing each time you take yourself too seriously. The world does not revolve around your ego conscious being. Truthfully, the world awaits only your awareness of the Truth you are, and not some crazy idea you have about yourself. Be aware of the times you engage with self-importance and then release your feelings and unfounded beliefs and opinions into the ethers of laughter and goodness. Just stay aware and respond with Wisdom.

Chapter Nine, Principle Seven: I am my brother's brother, not my brother's keeper.

Life affords us with ample opportunity to practice applying divine consciousness as the corrective value. As you traverse through each day, stay alert to anything you see as spiritually erroneous, even literally erroneous, like a misspoken word or unfortunate response to the call for Love. Immediately take on your responsibility to shift the erroneous behavior to the Truth. See it merely as not being of God, not inhabiting divine consciousness, and then correct it to inhabiting divine consciousness—but only inwardly, for yourself. There is no need to correct anything in anyone else; there is only the need to correct erroneous perceptions within you, shifting from how you formerly saw them to the Truth.

This is such a simple, yet commanding, process. Stay aware of resonance within, for resonance will inform you in each instance of what is correct spiritually. Once there, in divine consciousness, imbed that Wisdom indelibly in your heart and daily practice. The more you practice this the more you will exercise Life out of divine consciousness. And the less you will be tempted to correct the world. In fact, you *are* correcting the Universe as you abide in divine consciousness. Each time you apply this to some situation or observation, all are lifted along with you. Each may not be lifted exactly like you are, but upliftment need not be identical in order to be effective.

So, practice observing all around you, as well as all you feel within you, throughout each day. In each instance, respond to all that resonates out of kinship with what you gnow to be the Truth. That is all there is to it. Bottom line, there is not more to Life than this. Life is all about resting in the conscious awareness of Wisdom. And all the rest is given unto us as we need it—from that very same Source—bit-by-bit, step after step, on our path of spiritual authenticity.

Endnotes

This book was formed originally with another publisher under the title, *HAVE YOU FORGOTTEN?* The contract with that publisher has been properly terminated and this book represents a major revision of the original.

Should you become interested in an even deeper investigation into metaphysical treatment, it is suggested you invest some energy engaging with the following two sources: *Science and Health; With Key to the Scriptures,* by Mary Baker Eddy, and *The Early Years; The 1932-1946 Letters of Joel S. Goldsmith,* by Joel S. Goldsmith. In addition, you will find more spiritually referenced definitions of words in *Webster's New Universal Unabridged Dictionary* than in most other sources of this nature, and *The Metaphysical Bible Dictionary* is also a marvelous source of inspiration.

Elements cited and/or paraphrased can be found in the following documents, as well as in those citations noted at the time of their inclusion in the text itself:

All quotes or paraphrases attributed to Jesus can be found in the Gospels contained in The New Jerusalem Bible; mostly from the Gospel of John, but found also in the Gospels of Matthew, Mark, and Luke.

Mission and Style of the Arkansas Metaphysical Society, from the annals thereof.

Quotes from sayings of friends, by their permission.

Other quotes: through various search engines on Internet.

W. Stuart Booth, "Overcoming Ruminations," *Healing Thoughts,* the journal of The Plainfield Christian Science Church, Plainfield, NJ. Number 121, November 2007.

Ralph Waldo Emerson, "Self-Reliance," found in *Ralph Waldo Emerson: Essays and Journals.* Nelson Doubleday, Inc., 1968.

Joel A. Goldsmith, *Consciousness Transformed.* Atlanta,

Georgia: Acropolis Books, Inc., 1998.

William Roedel Rathvon, Vol. I: *Association Addresses (1912-1938)*. Santa Clara, CA: The Bookmark, 2007.

Jim Young, *The Creation Spirit: Expressing Your Divinity in Everyday Life*. New York: iUniverse, Inc., 2006.

Jim Young, *A Labor of Love: Weaving Your Own Virgin Birth on the Loom of Life*. New York: iUniverse, Inc., 2006.

Jim Young, *What If? Changing Your Life to Fit Your Truth*. New York: iUniverse, Inc., 2006.

Jim Young, *Only Mind Matters: Emerging From the Waters of Symbolic Meaning*. New York: iUniverse, 2007

"Once when Jesus was attempting to explain a spiritual truth, His disciples complained because the teaching was difficult. They were looking through a filter of limited thinking. He was teaching them about spiritual insight that was beyond what they were comprehending in the physical world. It was a message of 'spirit and life.'"

Daily Word, Oct. 2008, p. 40

B O O K S

O is a symbol of the world, of oneness and unity. In different cultures it also means the "eye," symbolizing knowledge and insight. We aim to publish books that are accessible, constructive and that challenge accepted opinion, both that of academia and the "moral majority."

Our books are available in all good English language bookstores worldwide. If you don't see the book on the shelves ask the bookstore to order it for you, quoting the ISBN number and title. Alternatively you can order online (all major online retail sites carry our titles) or contact the distributor in the relevant country, listed on the copyright page.

See our website www.o-books.net for a full list of over 500 titles, growing by 100 a year.

And tune in to myspiritradio.com for our book review radio show, hosted by June-Elleni Laine, where you can listen to the authors discussing their books.